CONTENTS

Foreword ....Page   v
Preface ....Page   xi

Part One: A Losing Battle

Chapter One:
    A Personal Odyssey.............................Page   3
Chapter Two:
    Unseen Warfare................................Page   17
Chapter Three:
    Unseen Personal Enemies ....Page   27

Part Two: Back to the Basics

Chapter Four:
    The Holy Trinity..............................Page   39
Chapter Five:
    The Word Became Flesh ....Page   61
Chapter Six:
    I Believe in the Remission of Sins ....Page   78
Chapter Seven:
    Divine Energy for Human Living ....Page   96
Chapter Eight:
    The Sword in the Fire ....Page   113
Chapter Nine:
    Personal Communion with the Personal God ..Page 130

Part Three: Christ Our Victory

Chapter Ten:
    The Action Plan...............................Page   143
Chapter Eleven:
    A Battle Call ....Page   156

Whenever you wish to make a beginning in some good work, first prepare yourself for the temptations that will come upon you, and do not doubt the truth. For it is the enemy's custom, whenever he sees a man beginning a good mode of life with fervent faith, to confront him with diverse and fearful temptations, so that he should be afraid, his good intention should be chilled, and he should lack the fervor to undertake that God-pleasing work.

It is not that our adversary has such power (for then no one could ever do good), but God concedes it to him, as we have learned with the righteous Job.

Therefore prepare yourself manfully to encounter the temptations which are brought against the virtues, and then begin to practice them. For if you have not prepared yourself beforehand to meet temptations, then refrain from practicing virtues.

—Saint Isaac the Syrian, 7th Century

FOREWORD

There is a great howling desert, an arid place of confusion and spiritual failure; it is a place in which many of us who have tried to be faithful Protestant Christians have lived in sorrow. This desert was once a garden irrigated by the mighty rivers of holy Tradition and authentic New Testament spirituality, a garden hedged in by a great protective barrier of true theology. Not subjective experiential modern "theology," but living doctrine founded on the revealed Word of God, given to human beings by God through the Scriptures, by the Son of God, and by the Apostolic faith of the historic Church defended by the blood of the martyrs.

Once, not long ago, in near despair, I believed that the age of historic Christianity was perhaps only a thing of the dimly remembered past. I believed that as far as spiritual truth went, it was now every man and woman for themselves, alone, islands, each splendidly isolated—not only from past Christian tradition—but from any present sense of spiritual community as well. I believed that I was alone in my Christian walk, alone with the Bible, *sola scriptura*, my conscience, and God—if God even noticed, that is. Since I am a sinner, weak and vacillating in my faith, I failed as a Christian. For as author and friend Jon Braun writes: "It is hard to fight when you don't understand what's going on." And I might add it's

impossible to pull yourself up by your own spiritual boot-
straps!

In His infinite mercy, the Lord gently led me out of the
"desert" of modern Protestant evangelical Christianity and
brought me to the threshold of the ancient garden I once
believed to be long gone. Here I have discovered a living holy
Tradition that does not demand I go it alone but rather offers
practical, spiritual, communitarian help.

Overgrown, forgotten, yet intact, the historic Orthodox
Church is alive and well. The glorious, sure, and certain faith
of the Fathers is still with us! On December 16, 1990, I was
chrismated (joined) into the Orthodox Church. It was a
coming home, a cause for celebration and hope. At long last
I had been given weapons of sacrament, faith, and tradition
with which to do spiritual battle. I was no longer trying to go
it alone.

My own dissatisfaction with the simplistic and reduction-
ist Protestant shadow that today passes for a sort of imitation
Christianity, had turned from sorrow to joy. And instead of
bitterness I began to wish that someone would reach out to
others even as I had been touched. I came to realize that
Christianity was not broken but that my disillusionment and
spiritual failure had come from my own wrong ideas about the
location of true faith. Jon Braun writes: ". . . where do such
misinformed ideas originate? Laziness, ignorance, lack of
faith, confused thinking, and lack of genuine experience of
God. . . ." Jon Braun could be describing me and the cheap
grace that masquerades as salvation in much of the impover-
ished Christian world today. As he writes: "The Christian life
is not just 'knowing Jesus.' To reduce things down that far
cuts spiritual living into spiritual ribbons."

Yet for most of us who come from various Protestant backgrounds, our own personal "deserts" of spiritual failure, that we have experienced and that formed our "Christianity," have consisted of little more than "just knowing Jesus," in the manner Jon Braun describes. The problem with such a shallow idea of salvation is that it is wrong! Wrong not only theologically, but wrong also in view of the historic witness of the Church which has never preached salvation is a magical or mantra-like, one-time affair. Instead the True Church has explained salvation as a journey.

As readers of this invaluable book will learn, true salvation starts with a willingness to repent of our folly and follow true ideas, not just subjective "feelings." Our religious understanding has consisted too often of late of little more than a subjective and forlorn hope that our "born-again" experience is sufficient to see us through the trials and temptations of this life. Our experiential Protestant "desert" is such an all-pervasive, monolithic culture that, within it, we Protestants never dreamed that there was still a faith both sure and "primitive"—close to the early Church—vibrant and true, of which it could be accurately proclaimed, "This is the faith of the Fathers; this is the doctrine of the Apostles!" Yet once it was precisely with such red-blooded confidence that the Church did proclaim its eternal and sacramental truth. Dare I say of the book by Jon Braun that the contents herein do not represent a mere "opinion," but indeed the "faith of the Fathers"?

Not a moment too soon does Jon Braun write: "Spiritual growth stops with the cessation of repentance." Not a moment too soon, because many a lonely, shepherdless Protestant Christian has been robbed of the very tools of grace by which he or she can be *brought* to true repentance—to a *daily* starting over. True spiritual growth has indeed stopped for countless thousands of such persons mainly because of the very sort of "misinformed...lack of faith" Braun seeks to correct with this timely book.

This book is a life line—a ray of hope that comes from the center of the ancient and verdant garden of Apostolic faith. It is a beacon that, if followed, will lead the weary Christian traveler who is sick and tired of going it alone back to that good land that he has almost despaired of ever reaching.

How do we win our personal war against temptation? How do we turn our failure to *be* Christians—rather than simply *to become* Christians—into true spiritual triumph against our merciless passions and the temptations of the demons? How, in short, do we achieve "union with Christ"? Jon Braun answers these and other pressing practical questions in this well-written, easily understandable book and shows us that, "we are to be . . . co-operators with God. We need to know what God expects from us in [our] spiritual battle."

Jon Braun is a priest and a true theologian—in other words, a man of prayer. Those who read this book will find that he has abandoned what he rightly brands "pat answers for victorious living," and instead marks a *practical* path by which we can return to the beginning of things—to innocence and a childlike faith.

This indeed is a "back to basics" book. The basics presented herein are not, however, the invention of one man, nor are they found only in this book; they are rather a reflection of the faith and worship of the historic Church! Jon Braun is not reinventing the wheel. Instead, he is leading us to a rediscovery of the wheel of faith long since lost, squandered, or abandoned. He is picking it up, dusting it off, and setting it aright.

Just as my friend Jon Braun patiently took time to explain many things to me and answer many questions which I asked him personally regarding the Orthodox Faith, so through these pages he extends his patience and compassion to a wider audience and builds what I feel is a vital and important bridge between the present age of misguided ideas and those eternal truths which we have squandered to our loss. May God bless him for writing, and bless those who read what is contained herein. And may God lead you across the bridge Jon Braun has crafted to a true and good land of green pastures and still waters.

JOHN FRANCIS SCHAEFFER
(A.K.A. FRANKY SCHAEFFER)
JUNE, 1991

PREFACE

First, this is a book about spiritual warfare. It is intended to be a bridge—a bridge to help Protestant Christians understand and become familiar with historic Orthodox Christianity. While it is written particularly for Protestant Christians by an Orthodox pastor, it is my hope that many Orthodox believers will benefit from their reading of the book also.

It has been my experience that there are millions of committed Christians in Protestant Churches who sincerely love God with all their hearts but who also have discovered that the Christian life is often a battle—a battle against sin. They are unreservedly dedicated to Christ, but are frustrated because they aren't winning what they believe should be their share of those spiritual wars. It is my conviction that in the depth of Orthodox theology and spirituality, new—actually, old—answers may be found. For all true Christians recognize truth when they hear it, and it is my hope that the truth of the Orthodox Faith will come through in this book.

Let me assure you, I understand the frustration of losing out in spiritual war!

Beginning in my teens, I searched for answers to success in that battle. The search led in some directions I did not anticipate. For instance, I think it is fair to say that my going from being a Protestant evangelical pastor and collegiate

evangelist to an Orthodox priest could not have been anticipated by anyone, but that is where God so clearly brought me.
It was in discovering the historic Orthodox Faith I found the
working answers, the answers for which I had searched for so
long. I don't mean to imply I win every battle today, but I have
discovered "a great cloud of witnesses" who won not only
many but most of the battles, and what they said, wrote, and
did has been of the utmost encouragement to me.

Secondly, this is a book about theology.

The theme of the book is spiritual warfare, but that is not
its only purpose. The scope and intention go considerably
beyond that to the arena of sound theology. And I hope this
theology will build a bridge not only to historic Christian
spirituality for those intent on winning the spiritual war, but
that it will draw readers into a love for *doctrine* as well. My
aim is to pass on this theology in lay language.

Now and then, you will still hear the naive allegation that
study of theology is synonymous with spiritual deadness.
True doctrine never produces death, because truth cannot
produce death. It brings us life! Correct doctrine about the
Holy Trinity, the incarnation of Christ, and our salvation are
vitally important to Christian living. So I have sought here to
take the historic teaching of the Church on these matters and
to make them understandable, interesting, and applicable to
the average Christian.

This book has come about in essentially three phases: I
began teaching about the truths of forgiveness and my early
spiritual journey while working with Campus Crusade for
Christ. A clearer understanding of the Holy Trinity, the
incarnation, and our union with Christ was set forth, in part, in
my earlier volume, *It Ain't Gonna Reign No More*, published

by Thomas Nelson, Inc. Finally, a practical understanding of how God's uncreated energies work in our lives, especially when it comes to winning at spiritual warfare, has been added as a result of ten years of maturity in the study of Orthodox spirituality.

Isaac the Syrian once said, "It is as shameful for lovers of the flesh and the belly to search out spiritual things as it is for a harlot to discourse on chastity." With that in mind, I cautiously risk publication of this volume.

PART I

A LOSING BATTLE

Chapter One

A PERSONAL ODYSSEY

Illumine our hearts, O Master who loves mankind, with the pure light of Your divine knowledge, and open the eyes of our mind to the understanding of Your gospel teachings. Implant in us also the fear of Your blessed commandments, that trampling down all fleshly desires, we enter into a spiritual manner of living, both thinking and doing such things as are pleasing unto You. For You are the illumination of our souls and bodies, O Christ, our God. —A prayer before the reading of the Gospel

From a personal point of view, that summer high-school conference at a facility nestled in the Santa Cruz mountains of California could hardly have been more significant. It was the occasion for my first conscious step on a spiritual pilgrimage that would mark the direction of my life from then until now. Mine was an intensely personal quest to discover how to live my life the way God intended human life to be lived.

I have no doubt that there are literally millions of Christians who deeply desire to live as God purposed them to live but who, as I, have been exasperated by repeatedly frustrating dead-ends and unexpected detours in their spiritual journey. I do not desire that anyone share every step of my way. God forbid! But as for the end of my journey to the historic Orthodox Church, I commend it to everyone who desires to live for God. Because in this exceedingly unexpected place, the desire of the heart can find fulfillment.

As my own journey began, I was one of the six or seven hundred high-school young people who attended that summer conference. Several unusually capable speakers challenged us to commit our lives unreservedly to Christ and to live for Him. The majority of us had some working knowledge of what that meant. As the week progressed, there was a swell of excitement among us. To use a contemporary expression, most of us were becoming "turned on" to Christ.

What I was hearing then was not completely new to me. For my introduction to the Christian life had begun in early childhood. It was one of the first things I was taught by my devotedly Christian parents. Their instruction was intense— and it wasn't on Sunday only, but virtually *every* day.

But now, at the conference, I was hearing these same things in an environment that couldn't be duplicated in our home, or even at the old Knox Presbyterian Church where my father was pastor. Those kids and the persuasive speakers combined to make becoming a more deeply committed Christian exceptionally attractive for me.

I was already thoroughly convinced about Christ. But this was a time of extraordinary spiritual enthusiasm. I had never experienced anything quite like it. I also possessed an intense yearning for a quality of life different from what I saw in myself, something I thought I saw in others around me, both young and old. There was a way God wanted people to live, and I wanted to live that way. If commitment to Christ was the way to that life, I was prepared to make it.

Though still young, I had a fairly clear understanding of such a commitment.

First, I knew it involved a relationship with God. That relationship assumed the need for getting to know God, personally. I didn't expect that to happen in an instant, by the way. I was aware it didn't work that way. There had to be a growing knowledge of Him, for a relationship with God had to involve progress.

Second, I recognized that the bottom line of such a commitment involved a desire to do God's will in all things, no matter the cost.

Third, at least in my mind, I realized I could not live this way in my own strength. I needed God to help me, to give me His power. I recognized there was a significant degree of emotional appeal in what was being said. But inside, I knew the Christian life was not to be lived out on a "feelings" basis as an emotional high. The strength to live it must come from God.

It was, as I recall, on the fourth evening of the conference that I timidly slipped up to one of the leaders to tell him of my decision to follow Christ's footsteps. He insistently encouraged me to share my new commitment to live for the Lord publicly before the whole group. A time was provided each day for such a witness to be made, and I resolved to do so.

It took me two more days, though, to muster enough courage to express my resolution publicly! I was totally petrified of the huge group of kids, but I was determined nothing would prevent me. In a trembling, cracking, still-changing voice, I announced that I was totally "sold-out" to Christ and would follow Him forever, no matter the cost.

Words cannot describe the joy and excitement which welled up in me during the next hours and days. I was persuaded no power on earth could hinder my resolve. I had entered upon what I believed to be a spiritual manner of living, a life of knowing God and doing His will. Nothing I had ever known compared to it.

But my enthusiasm wasn't going to stay that high for long.

Do you recall the first time it dawned on you this matter of living as a Christian wasn't going to be easy? Well I do. And vividly!

The Spiritual Slump

I first noticed the "slump" coming on about three weeks after the conference. It baffled me. I didn't want my spiritual fervor to die out. I genuinely desired to live for God, but something was happening within me I couldn't explain, and it was hindering my spiritual progress.

It focused on the standard daily teenage sins and temptations I encountered: bad thoughts, temper-tantrums, desire to be popular, fantasies. I began capitulating to some of them with alarming predictability. The guilt and grief that followed my falls were devastating to me. I wanted to do what I believed God wanted me to do, but I seemed powerless to live that way, at least in some of these areas.

Frustrated? You better believe it! After making that confident, definite, public affirmation about following Christ, here I was both thinking and doing things I knew both He and I disapproved of—no way were they the will of God.

6

Yet in spite of my efforts to the contrary, I continued plunging down from my spiritual high until I bottomed out at a consistently low spiritual plateau. My failure was to be the source of fervent searching for years to come. And to make matters worse, the mega-joy I had experienced those first days after my resolution to follow Christ was a rapidly fading memory. I felt helpless to halt the process.

Slowly and steadily, I became conscious of a spiritual war deep within me. The dark side on the line of demarcation was trying to keep me from doing and being what I sincerely wanted to do and be. The other side was drawing me on to follow Christ. I read from the Apostle Paul in Galatians 5:17, "For the flesh lusts against the Spirit, and the Spirit against the flesh; and these are contrary to one another, so that you do not do the things that you wish." That I understood!

Spiritual warfare was all new to me then. And I had no idea this inner struggle was only the beginning stage of a larger campaign. In the years to come, the smell of smoke, as it were, of those battles would become very familiar.

The *fact* of the conflict didn't really depress me. There was even challenge in that. But it was my *always* getting whipped that became such a source of discouragement. I wanted to win some of those battles!

Don't misunderstand. Had I known how long, tough, and discouraging the course would be during the years to follow, I still would have made my same choice to follow Christ. And I would make it again today. (In fact I do, every day of my life!)

The First of Many New Beginnings

Exactly one year later I was introduced to the phenomenon many Christians have encountered: the "re-dedication" cycle.

Enter the mountain-top experience! The occasion for this was my return to the conference I'd been to the year before. Responding anew to a fresh challenge from fresh speakers to remake the same commitment to God I made the previous summer, I was delighted to discover the spiritual fervor returning with most of its vivid excitement.

But so did the subsequent slump with its numbing spiritual chill.

That on-again off-again state became the norm of my life as a young Christian. And though it was *characteristic* of my experience, I could not help but reject it as being normative. If that were all there was to be, it would mean God was capricious—a spiritual tease.

I knew that was impossible. The problem must lie with me.

On the one hand, I still had a burning desire to do the will of God. But I was constantly failing. I understood something of the mercy and forgiveness of God, and that was a source of moderate comfort.

But on the other hand I longed for more than forgiveness for my failures. I wanted to *stop* failing! I virtually ached to live a life that would both honor Christ and satisfy myself. Something was very wrong somewhere. A vital piece, or pieces, of the fullness of Christianity had to be missing. I was determined to find what was missing and get the problem fixed.

Even before age fourteen, long before, I had been convinced that my calling in life was to serve God in the Christian ministry. Never once did I seriously consider anything else. My conference experiences merely fortified that conviction. I pursued the necessary schooling, and at twenty-four I was ordained to the Christian ministry. Though I set out expectantly to serve Christ faithfully, I was still aggressively seeking a solution to inconsistent spiritual living. That's a trying situation for a young minister!

Many Shortcuts, No Solutions

It wasn't that I didn't seek help in all of this. I approached just about anyone and everyone who appeared able to help. And I tested most of their recommendations, usually with at least a modicum of immediate effect. But that itself was a problem; the relief was *always* just temporary. After an initial burst of success, the slump set in again.

I had many counselors who were positive they had the sure "key" to effective Christian living. As I look back, most of their strategies promising spiritual consistency were actually made up of pieces of truth. But by themselves, those pieces didn't work as promised.

It's profitable to summarize those keys. They're the standard fare. Possibly you've tried some—or all—of them, and perhaps you have been crash landing, too.

The "read the Bible and pray" key

Daily Bible reading and prayer was the first key to be offered to me. Results were guaranteed. I would become a young man of God, I was assured, if only I were consistent at reading the Bible and praying. "How can a young man cleanse his way? By taking heed according to Your word" (Psalm 119:9), I was quoted. "Heed" equaled "read." And prayer was to be my communication link with God.

New enthusiastic confidence prompted me to pursue both, and the solution seemed plausible enough. So I read and read, and I prayed and prayed. I learned many things about the Bible and received some genuine answers to prayer. But to my great disappointment, this didn't stop the yo-yo effect in my life as a Christian.

I recognized then, as I do still, that sincere Bible reading and earnest prayer are commendable, proper, and helpful for Christian living. But in themselves they do not, they cannot, provide the power for spiritual life. The Bible never makes that claim for itself. And though surely there is communion with God in prayer, effective prayer is no simple matter.

What really baffled me, however, was that as I pursued Bible study and prayer, the spiritual tug-of-war within me actually grew more intense. And I got worse! My resolve to follow God didn't weaken, but my efforts to live for God did. That distressed me. It wasn't the fault of the Bible, prayer, or God. The fault was mine. But I was somehow unenlightened, powerless to improve.

The "baptism of the Holy Spirit" key

Just at that time the charismatic movement was emerging on the West Coast. It brought a needed emphasis on the Holy Spirit many had neglected. Impressed with what I saw, I began to meet some people involved in the movement. Their emphasis would become the second key to the Christian life offered to me.

"If you are going to live for God," they said, "you must be filled with the Holy Spirit." Now it doesn't require a high degree of spiritual insight to figure out that apart from the Holy Spirit there is no way to effectively live the Christian life. As a famous Russian Christian of the last century, Saint Seraphim of Sarov, continually stressed, "The true end of the Christian life is the acquisition of the Holy Spirit." I could grasp that, and I agreed with it.

But always up for grabs in the charismatic movement were: 1) who the Holy Spirit is, and 2) what it means to be filled with the Holy Spirit. These are questions of no small degree of gravity. Spiritual life and health rest upon them. There is little room for error here. Talking about the Holy Spirit doesn't bring anyone into a proper relationship with the Holy Spirit. Christian history is filled with examples of people who constantly stressed the Holy Spirit, but erred greatly: Simon the Sorcerer was one, a second century heretic named Montanus another.

Then there was the infighting among Christians as to the correct "experience" with the Spirit. Some said it was a baptism. Others insisted it was a filling. There were those who contended you had to speak in tongues to be filled with the Holy Spirit. Some said only faith was needed. In the face of endless arguments and disputes, there came much confusion and division.

Preaching about the Holy Spirit is important and often impressive. It touches the heart strings of the Christian. But the words need to be true and the experience genuine. There are religious experiences which are true and religious experiences which are false. A false religious experience of the baptism or filling of the Holy Spirit, even when accompanied with such signs as speaking in tongues, not only will fail to be helpful to consistent godly Christian living, but it may actually be counter-productive and eventually very damaging. You undoubtedly know of several ex-charismatics who are no longer on the scene.

One piece that didn't fit was the spoken, or sometimes tacit, assertion that *all that is needed* for spiritual living is a particular experience labeled "being filled with the Holy

Spirit." It grieves me deeply when I hear so much radio and television preaching on this kind of thing. It doesn't work. It can't sustain you to the finish-line of this life. Yes, you need the Holy Spirit, but you need Him in the context of the whole of a life God has provided for the Christian. Isolate a part of that provision, individualize it and make it all encompassing, and the whole of the Christian life is seriously sabotaged.

It wasn't that I gained nothing from seeking the Holy Spirit. But the strength I sought for living the life I read about from Christ and the Apostles in the Bible wasn't to be found in pursuing the Holy Spirit the way this was being presented. It sounded so good, but it didn't deliver. Mind you, it wasn't that the Holy Spirit couldn't deliver. Rather, the teachings lacked "context"—and some even contained heresy. Further, as the years progressed, it was evident that those who were so zealous for the charismatic movement were not gaining that for which even they were seeking.

The "vocal witness for Christ" key

Disappointed in the charismatic movement, I reached out for a third key, one that was to prove very exciting—though it also failed to yield the desired result.

"If you are not actively telling others about Christ," I was informed, "you are not doing the will of God, and this will cause spiritual inconsistency." Well, I surely wasn't an active witness for Christ, and the idea of my silence definitely sounded an alarm as a possible cause of my weakness as a Christian. If I was being disobedient to God in not being a verbal witness for Christ, that must be remedied.

I wholeheartedly accepted the challenge to witness for Christ. In the years that followed I spoke to many thousands of people about Christ—one on one, and in groups. By anyone's standards, I was a zealous, active witness for Christ, and people did respond to God as a result of that proclamation.

I learned some effective means of communicating the gospel, and I still believe there is a proper place for a verbal witness to Christ. But being an active Christian witness made zero impact on the matter of my spiritual consistency. The discrepancy between my own Christian experience, and the experience in Christ which I was promising to others, became increasingly apparent to me. Such inconsistency creates an unnerving paradox for any preacher!

But by far the most discouraging result of the verbal witness was that many of those who seriously responded to the message soon got caught up in the same frustration in which I was ensnared. And they looked to me for help in overcoming their spiritual struggles!

"Telling everybody" (even for those of us who are called to do it) as a method of finding personal spiritual stability is another faulty key. Evangelism is not done for the purpose of becoming more spiritual. It's a bad use of a good thing, like trying to saw through nails with a wood saw.

The "He will do it all through you" key

As a young minister, I heard a man exclaim, "The Christian life is not a hard life to live; it's impossible. Only Christ can live it, and He will live it in you."

According to this fourth key, you don't have to do anything at all to win the spiritual battles. In fact, you step aside. Christ Himself will do everything He wants in and through you. All you have to do is have faith and be the willing vehicle through which He can work.

The scheme appeared to be bolstered by several passages in the Scriptures, provided you ignored or explained away several other passages which contradict it. (Why mess up a good deal with all the facts?) I set out on this course expecting it would work. It didn't.

This key turned out to be a program of manipulation of biblical data. It isn't that the data is bad, it's the poor interpretation of it. The historic substance is not there. It was a pleasant "mind-trip," but useless under pressure.

The fact that I, and so many others, have locked into such overstatement and spiritual passivism only points out the acute frustration we experience when we cannot produce lasting fruit in our spiritual lives. Desperate people will believe and venture out on almost anything that promises to deliver spiritual success.

It must also be said here, as with the other keys we've discussed, that there was a measure of truth in the proposal. It wasn't that it was all wrong. It simply wasn't all right! Christ does work in us. But we must work, too, or nothing will be forthcoming from our lives. I can't remember how often in those days the Scripture was quoted, "For it is God who works in you both to will and to do for His good pleasure" (Philippians 2:13). But seldom was the immediately preceding verse quoted, "Therefore . . . work out your own salvation with fear and trembling." In doing the will of God, our work is ineffective without His working in us. But we do work effectively if God is at work within us.

Sincere But Misguided

Most of the people offering these keys were, I am convinced, truly sincere in promoting their particular programs.

But as time passed and I became personally acquainted with people who espoused each of these keys, I discovered that not only did their solutions not work for me, but they were not working for them either.

In private, we admitted our discouraging spiritual struggles, but in public the respective messages were expounded with unshakable confidence. It must be said emphatically that we did have a true Christian experience—there was some reality, some fulfillment. But we knew our experience was not commensurate with what we read about in the Scriptures.

Light at the End of the Tunnel

In spite of all the frustration, there was never a time when I doubted I would somehow find that for which I longed. With a number of close friends and "traveling companions" on the same journey, I began to search into the early history of the Church to find if others had found answers to the same questions I had. We had learned the Scriptures. This time, we wanted to see what other Christians had done with those same passages of Scriptures that we had come to know and love.

Not too far into our investigation, we were shocked to discover there were whole chapters, as it were, of Church history with which we were totally unfamiliar. And in our quest to get to the bottom of what was missing, we made a monumental discovery.

That discovery was the historic Orthodox Church.

We didn't even know it still existed. But we were thrilled to find there had been a time in the history of Christianity when what we sought and believed to be normative—the consistent spiritual life—actually *was* normative. Our forbearers had asked the same questions we had, used the same Book, but they had answers that not only made sense, *they worked!* There were no clever formulas, no keys. Rather they possessed an understanding of the Christian life and how it is to be lived. The life they spoke of was dynamic—and wholly different from anything to which we had ever been exposed. Scriptures we had passed over, because we couldn't fit them into our understanding, sprang to life.

And so did we.

The chapters which follow share what it was we discovered, and how that discovery can touch the life of every seeking Christian.

Chapter Two

UNSEEN WARFARE

*For we do not wrestle against flesh and blood,
but against principalities, against powers,
against the rulers of the darkness of this age,
against spiritual hosts of wickedness in the
heavenly places.* —Ephesians 6:12

Have you ever experienced the temptation to commit a certain sin over and over, say the temptation to get angry in response to a certain repeated provocation, and you resisted successfully over and over? Then one day you succumbed. The next time you resisted successfully. Then you succumbed, resisted, succumbed, succumbed, succumbed. . . . Discouraging isn't it?

It's remarkable how quickly our determined resolve to truly live the Christian life weakens in the face of repeated temptations. We launch out with joy, determination, and faith to live for God. Then we are accosted by subtle temptations, which we may initially resist. But when these temptations reoccur frequently, we begin to succumb to some of them regularly.

It's not merely that we sin which discourages us so much.

Few of us ever anticipated "sinless perfection" in this life. It's when our surrender to certain temptations becomes predictable and habitual—like we're going to do it *every* time—that we become so disheartened. That is not the kind of Christianity we read of in the Scriptures, and it's not what we expected as we embarked on a course of living for Christ.

If we are serious about remedying our predictable tendency to commit certain sins over and over again, it will be extremely helpful to understand something of the nature of temptation and how to resist it. The purpose of this chapter is: 1) to focus on some things that go on within us in times of temptations, and 2) to explain why we easily fall prey to often repeated temptations.

The Reality of the Warfare

No serious Christian is exempt from temptation. And it should be obvious that repeated temptations are often accompanied by intense spiritual battles if we are going to resist them. About spiritual battles, we should know that: 1) we must be well prepared for them, 2) they need to be fiercely and thoughtfully fought, and 3) they can be won. Obviously Saint Paul had in mind the reality of spiritual battle when he wrote, "For we do not wrestle against flesh and blood, but against principalities, against powers, against the rulers of the darkness of this age, against spiritual hosts of wickedness in the heavenly places" (Ephesians 6:12).

Wrestle. What a graphic expression! Let me illustrate. All my kids competed in high school athletics. But without doubt, the most trying sport for me as a parent to watch my sons engage in was wrestling. Three of my five boys wrestled. It seemed to me as though I were out there on the mat myself—

at least my ego was. But it wasn't just the ego involvement that got to me. The exceptional effort the wrestlers exerted impressed me most. Strength, skill, and will against strength, skill, and will. If you've ever had much to do with wrestling, you know the resolve, endurance, and conditioning required to win a really close match.

That's also true for Christians in their wrestling with temptation. We're not talking about some easy contest. The "name it and claim it" programs for spiritual victory are a very bad joke! This is tough stuff. There are casualties. You must be prepared.

In my own Christian pilgrimage, it wasn't that no one warned me early on about spiritual conflict. Many did. But there was a glibness with which the subject was bantered about. The battles sounded real enough, but victory over temptation was made to appear so easy, so matter of fact, so . . . well, guaranteed.

Switch to boxing. I'll date myself with this illustration. Joe Louis was the heavyweight boxing champion of the world in the era when the United States was drawn into World War II. Victory over Japan seemed simple to my fourth grade mind. Send Joe Louis to knock out Emperor Hirohito, and it would all be over. I'm serious! You can imagine how difficult it was for me to understand America's early losses in the Pacific. I couldn't comprehend the realities of war, realities that included such grim matters as defeat and even death.

"Quote a Bible verse at the devil, and you'll defeat him like Jesus did in His temptation in the wilderness." "Just have faith, and you'll ward off all temptations." "Say a quick prayer, and you will be able to resist temptation." On many occasions I was offered these or similar "encouragements."

Though there is truth in the three pieces of advice I've just mentioned, spiritual wrestling matches aren't won by quotations and quips. Aware as I was there would be a war in the spiritual realm, I wasn't prepared to fight and win those battles. Expecting quick victory, *and using the quips*, I experienced humiliating defeat after defeat.

Know Your Enemy

Since you can't avoid temptations and the battles that often accompany them, it's useful to know at least what you're up against. Let us consider the process of defeat before we look at how to overcome temptations and evil doing. We need to know how it happens we turn from being resisters of temptation to being succumbers. Where, specifically, do we lose? What are these awesome powers with which we contend anyway?

In answering these questions I want to turn to the understanding of historic Orthodox Christianity and look to wisdom gained by men and women of God through long centuries of proven experience. Knowing the answers to these questions will not make you a winner in a single round in the conflict, but they will be very useful in helping you understand what you must do to become a winner.

The Process of Temptation

It's not unlikely you have at some time or another explained away a sin you committed with the half-hearted excuse, "I don't know why I did it. Something just seemed to get hold of me." Sound familiar?

How often have you experienced that enigmatic conflict down within you when you've been tempted—before you yielded to it? You felt as if you were in a whirlpool being sucked down into a sin you didn't really want to commit. You sensed that virtually the identical process had gone on in you before in the past, perhaps many times. And there seemed to be a power over you in that process you wanted to resist, but you steadily wore down. Then, after sinning, and keenly disappointed with yourself, you tried to determine what had happened. It wasn't clear. It was all so unreasonable. You did what you wanted to do, but you hadn't really wanted to do it. Right?

Saint Paul hit the nail on the head in explaining to the Romans, "For what I am doing I do not understand. For what I will to do, that I do not practice; but what I hate, that I do" (Romans 7:15).

There is a traceable process in all of this. There's a pattern in temptation, and you can learn it. You can see what's coming down, and be prepared to do something about it. Over the centuries, men and women who gave great attention to this have distilled that process. In summary, it boils down to six steps. [1]

Six steps in temptation
   Step 1—*Provocation.* This is, according to the eighth century writer, John of Damascus, "Simply a suggestion coming from the enemy, like 'do this' or 'do that,' such as our Lord Himself experienced when He heard the words, 'Command that these stones become bread' (Matthew 4:3)." There is nothing you can do to stop these suggestions. That's beyond

---

[1] I have opted here for outline purposes to use the summary given in *The Philokalia* (Faber and Faber, London, 1981) Volume I, pp. 365-366.

your power, and there is surely no sin involved. But you can—
and should—say a firm and immediate *no* to them. Saint
Mark the Ascetic says of this, "Like a mountain pass, the
experienced take control of it ahead of the enemy." Provocation is where the temptation process begins. There is no easier
place to put an end to it.

Step 2—*Momentary disturbance.* This almost explains
itself, doesn't it? You've felt it a thousand times. There's a
momentary uneasiness. It's like a warning light that comes on
as if saying, "Look out, here comes trouble. Be alert. Get your
guard up." You can pay attention to this warning or ignore it,
but it's there to get your attention.

Step 3—*Coupling.* Coupling is linking up with the
temptation in your mind. You decide to fool with the thing in
your head. John of Damascus defines it: "Coupling...means
dwelling on the thought and choosing deliberately to dally
with it in a pleasurable manner." He's speaking my language!
How many times I've done just that. Mind you, I haven't
committed any overt act yet. I'm just enjoying thinking about
the temptation—or maybe only thinking about thinking about
it. I can still resist, but I'm starting to weaken significantly.

Step 4—*Assent.* I've now *decided* to act on the temptation. I've done nothing yet, but it's as good as done. A bus
may run over me and prevent me from actually performing the
action, but I'm already guilty. I've sinned in my heart by
deciding to do so. In the light of this, consider Jesus'
statement, "But I say to you that whoever looks at a woman to
lust for her has already committed adultery with her in his
heart" (Matthew 5:28).

Step 5—*Prepossession.* Simply put, prepossession has
occurred when you've fallen to the same temptation so many

times your "memory banks" and you are beginning to be locked into it. You fight, but virtually always lose. You've become predisposed to committing this particular sin. Theoretically, you still have free will, and you're still accountable for committing the sin, but your free will is about as effective in wrestling against the particular temptation as a child in the ring with a skillful wrestler. You can pray, read the Bible, be baptized in the Holy Spirit, and witness to your faith daily, that is, employ all the "keys" from chapter one, and they won't help you resist that temptation. Those things may in fact be counter-productive because they aren't God's provision to resist sin, and you may be looking to them for help instead of doing what you ought to do.

Step 6—*Passion.* Give in often enough and you'll build a passion. Now you are passively predictable. You're consistently going to fall—it's almost as predictable as tomorrow's sunrise. Gluttony, immorality, anger, and pride are four examples of many sinful passions. We aren't born with these passions; we cultivate them, we acquire them. But once they are developed we are vulnerable because they can be set in motion in our thoughts not only by the devil, but by normal, natural desires, and even by past memories.

The compulsive power of passions

The process we've just considered describes the pathway, the process, of developing sinful passions. It's a demonstration of what the Scriptures speak of as "the law of sin." Saint Paul described it to the Romans this way: "But I see another law in my members, warring against the law of my mind, and bringing me into captivity to the law of sin which is in my members" (Romans 7:23). Passions take a vise-like grip on you.

Sinful passions are precisely what Paul had in mind when he said, "Therefore do not let sin reign in your mortal body, that you should obey it in its lusts" (Romans 6:12). "Lusts" and "passions" are one and the same thing. They are natural desires "run wild." *A Sinful passion is a desire inflamed and made predictable by the force of habit.*

Not all passions are sinful. You do need to eat, sleep, and drink. But sinful passions develop as you satisfy perfectly natural desires such as hunger, thirst, rest, or sex in a way contrary to, and harmful to, God's purpose. Think about hunger for a moment. Obviously there is no sin in being hungry or responding to it. Without those pangs you recognize as hunger, you might neglect eating and harm your body because of lack of nourishment. And it is not sin to eat what is appropriate—what you need. But you may choose to go beyond what is appropriate in satisfying your hunger. You feel hunger pangs, and so you eat quite enough to adequately satisfy your need. Then comes temptation: "That tasted great. You *need* more." You're well aware you don't need another bite. You're satisfied, just not stuffed. You're not under any great compulsion, but you go ahead and eat more.

The next time you go through the hunger satisfying process, your body seems to be crying out for more food after you've eaten all you need. You oblige. The process occurs again and again. A sinful passion is being cultivated. Gluttony becomes compulsive. Overeating becomes a habit for you, a passion. You just shovel the stuff in without even thinking about it.

That's the way it is with sinful passions. We are capable of developing many passions or lusts. These all begin with natural and normal desires not evil in themselves. But desires must be properly controlled or they may become sinful passions in us.

Those six steps make sense in helping us understand how we get caught up in habitual sin. We've all experienced all six. Obviously, the earlier we resist in the process, the easier it is to stand firm against temptation. The farther we let it go, the more captive we become—and, of course, the more defeated.

Unless sin, with its passions, is recognized and dealt with, we are by default its bewildered slaves, and consequently losers in spiritual conflict. The Apostle Paul warned the Romans, "Do you not know that to whom you present yourselves slaves to obey, you are that one's slaves whom you obey, whether of sin to death, or of obedience to righteousness?" (Romans 6:16).

Now a word of caution. We can't blame the compulsive power of passions for everything that happens to us and in us with respect to sin, and we must not use passions as an excuse for sinning. For one thing, this is not the only force at work against you. And for another, there is something you can do about your passions. We'll get to that shortly.

Passions don't sin. We do. Sinful passions don't develop themselves; we cultivate them, and we can stop the process by the provisions God has made for us in mercy and grace. But if we don't recognize the possibility of their presence, don't know how they work, and don't understand how they develop, we will more than likely be their dutiful—though perhaps ignorant—slaves.

The famous last words of the child of God who is naive about passions are, "But I thought a Christian was automatically freed from such things!"

In my own experience I was unable to deal well with repetitive temptations. I had no understanding of prepossession and passion. I treated each temptation as the first of its kind, and I got progressively weaker. It confused me that ungodly desires were not only still present with me, they were so often controlling me. I had been under the impression that once I was joined to Christ all such problems had been dealt with. But that is not what the Scriptures teach, nor the Fathers, and it is not true to Christian experience.

It's hard to fight when you don't understand what's going on. I knew I was fighting something, but I surely didn't know what it was, and I had no idea what to do. And so the forces of sin reigned altogether too often, making me their disheartened slave and a loser in spiritual conflict.

Chapter Three

UNSEEN PERSONAL ENEMIES

But suppose a man . . . is filled with desire to be free from the bondage of sin and has begun to work for it without delay. Even here the enemy does not leave him . . . The holy Fathers describe such a man as being under fire from all sides . . . From everywhere arrows speed towards him. Arrows from above are suggestions for excessive spiritual works, above his powers. Arrows from below are suggestions to reduce or even completely abandon such works through self-pity, negligence, and heedlessness. Arrows from the right are when, in connection with some right undertakings and works, the enemies lead a man into temptation and the danger of downfall. Arrows from the left are when the enemies present concrete temptations and draw a man towards sin. Arrows from the front are when the enemies tempt and disturb a man by thoughts of what is to come. Arrows from the rear are when they tempt him with memories of the past. —Saint John Chrysostom, 4th Century

We have considered both the process of temptation and the role of passions in habitual defeat in spiritual warfare. Now it is time to turn attention to the root of temptation—the devil. This we will do specifically as it relates to spiritual conflict.

It should come as no surprise to any Christian that the devil is a real and powerful enemy. Most of us know we have to deal with the devil, but there are several important things we can know about the devil to help us effectively war against him.

First, Satan is not just a force; he is a person who does possess power. Jesus called him the "ruler of this world" (John 12:31). Saint Paul named him "the prince of the power of the air" (Ephesians 2:2). Saint John explained that "the whole world lies under the sway of the wicked one" (I John 5:19). His domain overlaps our realm of existence. With Satan, the Christian deals with a foe who is jealous for the territory he claims as his own.

Second, the devil is a liar. The name devil means "deceiver." Jesus referred to Satan as the father of lies (John 8:44). Not only does the devil lie, he's clever at it. He disguises himself as an angel of light (II Corinthians 11:14). The red suit, horns, tail, and pitchfork image, for example, is one of his clever deceptions. Such fantasy leads people to view him as unreal, as a comic strip character. Even Christians can get the idea the devil is not much more than a joke. That's also part of his lie. He has a bag of tricks he'll use to fool even the wisest and most mature of Christians in order to catch them off guard.

Third, the devil does have access to people. Consider briefly some of the ways we know Satan has affected people, as recorded in Scripture:

- It was Satan who deceived Adam and Eve in the Garden (Genesis 3:1-6).
- Satan repeatedly smote Job of old, although it is clear in the biblical account that the Lord allowed this buffeting.
- The Prince of Persia, generally agreed by many biblical scholars to be a demonic personality, was temporarily able to block the way of a prayer being answered for three weeks (Daniel 10:13, 20; *cf*. Jude 9).
- Satan got the upper hand with Peter, causing him to try to deter Jesus from His resolve to go to the cross. The Lord had to reprimand him, saying, "Get thee behind me, Satan" (Matthew 16:23).
- It was the devil who entered into Judas, causing him to betray our Lord Jesus Christ (John 13:27).
- Satan filled the hearts of Ananias and his wife Sapphira to lie to the Apostles about their land-sale profits (Acts 5:3).

In these accounts, we gain insight into how and why Saint Peter could describe the devil as a "roaring lion, seeking whom he may devour" (I Peter 5:8).

Fourth, the devil doesn't operate by himself. He has hosts of demon-beings who are, as it were, on call to do his bidding (Ephesians 6:12). One of the most serious threats the demons pose to the Christian is that the demons supply food to our passions through the recollection of our own past sins—or even the sins of others. How often has some past incident when someone deeply offended you "come to your mind," and as you fed on it the passion of anger rose up within you with great strength. You asked yourself, "Where did that come from?" It is not unlikely that it was demonic prompting.

Back at the end of the sixth century, one victorious Christian, Saint John of the Ladder, wrote of the demons:

> The demons, murderers as they are, push us into sin. Or if they fail to do this, they get us to pass judgement on those who are sinning, so that they may defile us with the stain which we ourselves are condemning in another (*Ladder of Divine Ascent*, 10:11).

Fifth, Satan is a false accuser: "So the great dragon was cast out, that serpent of old, called the devil and Satan, who deceives the whole world; he was cast to the earth, and his angels were cast out with him. Then I heard a loud voice saying in heaven, 'Now salvation, and strength, and the kingdom of our God, and the power of His Christ have come, for the accuser of our brethren, who accused them before our God day and night, has been cast down' " (Revelation 12:9, 10). The name Satan means "accuser." His accusations are targeted at encumbering Christians with overwhelming guilt in order to discourage them from pursuing faithfulness to Christ.

Sixth, the devil has limitations. He is not God's counterpart. He is not omnipresent, everywhere, at all times. He isn't omniscient, all-knowing. His power does not begin to approach that of God's power. It is important you know these limitations. I've met people who are persuaded the devil is omnipresent, and they believe that every time they get an evil thought, Satan personally put it there. Certainly the devil could be indirectly involved, but it is impossible for him to be many places at once. A personal spiritual pride often lies at the base of seeing ourselves as so important that the devil himself is constantly and personally pushing temptation upon "poor little old me!"

The Devil and the Spiritual War

The "wiles of the devil" (Ephesians 6:11) are many. But in particular those with great experience say he employs four major points of attack against the Christian contestants in the spiritual war:

1) At the very beginning of a battle. Count on an attack from the devil any time you freshly resolve to embark on the path to pursue God—or do anything good, for that matter. God allows us to be tempted at such times, though not beyond what we are able (I Corinthians 10:13), in order that our faith and resolve be tested. It is extremely important that we begin everything with firm resolve and strong faith. Lacking these, we will be quickly "picked off" from the list of live contestants.

Think about it. How often have you decided you were going to take a new spiritual direction in your life—to pray consistently, clean up your language, resist lustful thoughts, or bear down in some spiritual discipline such as fasting—only to find temptations were far more frequent and stronger than they were before your decision. It was as though all hell broke loose against you, and you weren't ready for it. Spiritual living begins with faith and firm resolve. Then you go into battle. Not the other way around.

A further danger, particularly in the beginning stages of spiritual battle, is the subtle temptation of the devil to attempt too much. The devil can send good thoughts your way—things that are good to do, but they are way beyond your strength. You are tempted to pray too much. That's right, that is a temptation from the devil. Or you're tempted to engage in some essentially good spiritual ministry, but it's not the will of God for you, and it's not within your ability to do it. Thus you are defeated from the start, and it's a great victory for the devil because you've failed at something that looks so good and right.

2) As you feel the battle is successfully under way. If you survive the beginning skirmishes, you may find there is a period of little or no temptation, and you feel good about it. Watch out (Matthew 26:41)! Don't let your zeal drag—or as Paul says, "Not lagging in diligence, [be] fervent in spirit, serving the Lord" (Romans 12:11). The devil delights in having us settle into a little comfort, relax, or take life easy—even after a good start. Then he barrages us with temptations, and not being prepared to withstand, down we go to defeat.

Spiritual battle doesn't let up long. In that light comes Jesus' strong admonition to "watch and pray." What are we to watch for? Here are some examples John of the Ladder named:

> In all our actions in which we try to please God, the demons dig three pits for us. By the first, they endeavor to prevent any good at all from being done. By the second, after their first defeat, they try to secure that it should not be done according to the will of God. But when these rogues fail in this too, then, standing quietly before our soul, they praise us for living a thoroughly godly life. The first is to be opposed by zeal and fear of death, the second by obedience and humiliation, and the third by unceasing self-condemnation (*Ladder of Divine Ascent*, 26:7).

3) As you feel you're a winner. Let's assume you make a great start and you stay strong. But in the midst of that strength you begin to feel a measure of spiritual pride, as

though you are able to resist temptation in your own strength. "Hey, I'm really winning this war." This is extremely dangerous. There is no greater sin than pride. It is no doubt worse than succumbing to the temptation of the moment. Pride is the very original sin of the devil himself. As we resist temptation it is so easy to slip into the I-did-it-by-myself mode. That is spiritual death.

4) When your guard goes down after a long time in the battle. A fourth front of the devil's attack is to besiege you with fantasies—both of sinful things, and even of good things. Lust, greed, hatred, bitterness, misplaced zeal, and super-spirituality all fall into this class. It's devastating to the spiritual warrior because the unreal world of fantasy takes so much real energy and plunges the one who indulges in it into great depression and despair.

Combating the devil in these situations requires that at all times in spiritual battle you remember three things: a) You can do nothing apart from Christ (John 15:5), and that includes the resisting of temptation; b) It is imperative to keep God in the memory. That's the surest way to keep from pride. People with God in their memories are people that resist pride; and c) Remember also, "The Lord will fight for you" (Exodus 14:14).

Baptism—A Special Advantage

Many are unaware of a special advantage they have for overcoming Satan: baptism. Paul assured the Colossians, "The Father . . . has delivered us from the power of darkness and translated us into the kingdom of the Son of His love" (Colossians 1:12, 13). That transfer occurs in your baptism, and it is one reason baptism was such a key issue in the Church in New Testament times. Note there is not just a transfer to the kingdom of God's Son. There is also a deliverance from the power of darkness, and that includes the devil and his demons.

Recognizing this deliverance and transfer, the Orthodox baptismal service begins with an exorcism. That exorcism is followed by a three-fold renunciation of Satan, and the devil is actually spat upon! Here is part of one of the prayers of the exorcism:

> O Lord . . . , look upon Your servants . . . , and root out of them every operation of the devil. Rebuke the unclean spirits and expel them, cleansing the work of Your hands. And, using Your decisive might, beat down Satan under their feet, giving them victory over him, and over his unclean spirits.

Because God answers prayer, Christian experience needs to begin with prayer for victory over the devil. There is not the slightest possibility of victory apart from God. Even fleetingly entertaining the thought of victory over the devil on our own is in itself a victory of the devil over us.

A Plan of Attack

Our purpose in these last two chapters has not been to do an exhaustive study of sin, temptation, and the devil. For purposes of success in spiritual warfare, it has been necessary only to examine two inter-related aspects of what goes on inside of us as the war rages against us—temptation and how it works, and the devil himself and how he operates. These forces are powerful, but our situation is far from hopeless. There is a way to successfully do battle against them. But it takes knowledge of them, preparation for battle, and perhaps above all, some true knowledge of God.

It is to that basic knowledge we turn in the following section. I want to prepare you. This next section will require some thought and careful consideration. Gaining a basic understanding of who God is and what He has done for us is a challenging, yet wonderfully rewarding endeavor. So let me exhort you to read the following chapters carefully and with attention. Don't move on until you have the basics firmly in grasp. Once we "get a handle" on this pivotal information we will apply it practically to the spiritual warfare. You will understand by then how radically a proper understanding of the basics can affect both the outcome of that warfare and the day-to-day realities of the Christian life.

PART II

BACK TO THE BASICS

Chapter Four

THE HOLY TRINITY

When You, O Lord, were baptized in the Jordan, worship of the Trinity was revealed. For the voice of the Father came to testify, naming You His only beloved Son. And the Spirit, in the likeness of a dove, confirmed the certainty of that word. O Christ our God, You manifested Yourself, and enlightened the world. Glory be to You. —An Orthodox Epiphany Hymn

No one is ever consistently triumphant in the "unseen warfare" without a profound personal relationship with God. In this chapter we will consider doctrine *about* the God with whom that relationship must be established.

There are many "gods" in this world, and there are many people who mistake a false god for the true God. And many who have a false god are convinced they have the true Christian God. [I believe conviction isn't worth much unless it's true, no matter how sincerely people believe it.]

So how can I be sure I'm believing in and trusting in the true God? My opinion is as subject to error as anyone else's. To safeguard our consideration of the true God we sidestep personal opinion and speculation. Instead, our discussion will focus very specifically on the doctrine of God as it is understood in the historic Orthodox Church. In saying this, I want to be clear that God is certainly not the "property" of the Orthodox Church. And Orthodox Christians aren't the only people who love the true God. But historically speaking, it is the Orthodox Church which, in the face of a barrage of century upon century of error and heresy, hammered out the true doctrine of who God is.

Why do we need the Church's doctrine about God? Why not just read the Bible? Because that's overly simplistic, and it doesn't work. Literally thousands of heretics have claimed their teaching was straight from the Bible, and they were dead wrong—often leading others into great error and harm along with themselves. Nothing wrong with the Bible, mind you. Nothing at all! But because of faulty interpreters, basic boundaries have been set by the Church regarding what the Bible teaches about God. Cross over those boundaries, and you're in great danger of departing from the true God.

Knowing About God

There are some "ground rules" for knowing about God. First, knowledge about God doesn't guarantee any relationship with Him, but without it you have a guarantee your relationship with God will be shallow at best.

Second, it's foolish to capitulate to the frivolous notion that anything beyond the most elementary knowledge about God is not for your common, every-day Christian, but is only for professional theologians and select super-saints. Sincere Christians need sound doctrine concerning God.

It is common to hear insipid, unsubstantiated pronouncements like, "Doctrine divides and kills; it is our experience of Christ that gives unity and life." As if doctrine were some sinister culprit to be avoided at all costs! Such a notion may be religiously fashionable, but it is anything but the universal witness of the spiritual winners over the centuries. Besides, correct doctrine about God never has and never will kill anyone.

So where do such misinformed ideas originate?

Laziness, ignorance, lack of faith, confused thinking, and lack of genuine experience with God rank high on the list of possible roots of such reductionism. How absurd it would be for a husband to say, "I don't want to know anything about my wife. All I want is to relate to her as a person. I'm totally disinterested in her name, her parents and family, her background, her interests, her education, her likes and dislikes. These will only kill whatever relationship we might have together." Only a complete jerk would talk that way, and any potential relationship he might have with her would be doomed to be deficient. How much less will a relationship with God mature if we insist we do not want to know anything about Him! If you desire to know God personally, then desire to know anything and everything about Him you can.

God has made many things about Himself known to us. Part of that revelation is doctrinal knowledge, and with the help of God we can understand knowledge revealed about Him.

What is God's Name?

One of the very first things a young man wants to know about a young woman to whom he is attracted is her name. That's not silly or superfluous; that's proper. Likewise, one important place to begin in knowing God is to know His name. Actually, God has three names, for God is three persons, and each of those persons obviously has a personal name: Father, Son, and Holy Spirit.

"Wait! Don't you mean 'Creator, Redeemer, and Sustainer'? After all, this is the close of the twentieth century. Aren't terms like 'Father' and 'Son' likely to offend those who say such language is sexist and outmoded to describe the reality of who God is?"

It may be offensive to a few modernists, but the historic doctrine of the Trinity is and never could become irrelevant or outmoded. It represents the very basis for our understanding of God as He intended Himself to be revealed. If we don't know the three persons, Father, Son, and Holy Spirit, in the one God, we don't really know God at all. And far from being "sexist," this doctrine offers the greatest dignity possible to members of both sexes: the opportunity to truly know ourselves in the light of our Creator.

An Ancient and Modern Heresy

It is not incidental that the most serious doctrinal struggle the Church of Jesus Christ has ever known in all her history was over the question of the Trinity. A brief sketch of a piece of church history will show why it was important both then and now.

"There was a time when the Son of God was not." That was the bombshell hurled at the Church's recognized doctrine of the Trinity early in the fourth century A.D., by one Arius, a presbyter in the Church in Alexandria, Egypt. He insisted the Son of God was not truly God; He was merely the highest of created beings, and in that sense we could call Him *a god*. (That is virtually identical to the present day Jehovah's Witness heresy.)

You can well imagine the uproar this created! The conflict became so great it appeared for awhile the Church would be split apart. (Believe it or not, there were no significant divisions in all of Christendom at that time!) People divided up and took hard-line positions on the issue, and at first, no one would budge. There were charges and counter-charges of heresy. Accusations and anathemas were hurled about.

A great council of the whole Church finally had to be called in A.D. 325. It was convened in the city of Nicea near what is now Istanbul in Turkey. More than three hundred bishops gathered, plus hundreds of presbyters and deacons from all over the Roman Empire. The deliberations of the council lasted for months, with the goal of the discussion being the answer to the questions: What did Jesus Himself teach about this? What did the Apostles say? What do the Scriptures teach on this subject? And, what has the Church always believed about this? The results of all that discussion were consolidated in a concise creedal statement:

> We believe in one God the Father all-sovereign, maker of all things visible and invisible; and in one Lord Jesus Christ, the Son of God, begotten of the Father, only-begotten, that is, of the substance of the Father, God of God, Light of Light, True God of True God, begotten not made, of one substance with the Father, through whom all things were made, things in heaven and things on the earth; who for us men and for our salvation came down and was made flesh, and became man, suffered, and rose on the third day, ascended into the heavens, is coming to judge living and dead. And

in the Holy Spirit. And those that say, "There was when He was not," and, "Before He was begotten He was not," and that, "He came into being from what-is-not," or those that allege, that the Son of God is "Of another substance or essence" or "created," or "changeable," or "alterable," these the Catholic and Apostolic Church anathematizes.

This was not "new teaching" about God rising out of fourth-century Christian Greek philosophical speculation, as some have ignorantly—or wistfully—asserted. It was Arius who introduced new teaching. The people of God assembled at Nicea were specifically committed to *not* inventing a new doctrine about God, or about anything else for that matter. Their purpose was to determine what had *always been believed* about God on the basis of what was taught by Christ, His Apostles, the Scriptures, and the Church. They agreed this statement, this creed, said nothing more than that and nothing less.

Not only did they successfully settle the question, but they also made it clear that there are not options about believing in the Trinity. The Church, they said, anathematizes those who believe falsely about the Trinity. This word *anathema* is one tough word. It means "to curse." And where did the Church receive the authority to make such decisions? From Christ Himself whose body she is, and who gave to her the Holy Spirit to lead her into all truth.

Those people at Nicea didn't come up with a creed that was to gather dust over the centuries to follow, either. The creed they framed under the leading of the Holy Spirit has been acknowledged as true by virtually every segment of

Christendom in every age since. The Orthodox Church affirms it; the Roman Catholic Church affirms it; and almost all Protestant denominations affirm it. Even those Churches which claim they don't believe in creeds agree they believe what this creed says is true! The Nicene Creed (Nicene-Constantinopolitan Creed) is the single most agreed upon doctrinal statement in the history of Christianity. Here is a pronouncement for all professing Christians for all times.

Oh, there are some so-called Christians today, amongst them a few professional theologians, who don't believe in this doctrine. But whether or not they believe in it is quite beside the point when the question is raised as to whether the doctrine of the Trinity is part and parcel of historic Christianity. The historic faith of the Church and belief in the Holy Trinity are inseparable.

Understanding the Holy Trinity

A working definition of two words will be invaluable to our comprehension—both in mind and in heart—of the Trinity. Those two words are: *person* and *nature*. Take the second first.

Suppose you're walking by a pond one day and see two small boys gigging frogs. (For you uninitiated, that means to spear the little critters.) Such a scene might evoke many questions, but three in particular will help us understand the words person and nature. Question one is, "How do you distinguish the boys from the frogs?"

Nature

Contrary to the speculations of some who lack an appreciation for wet, dirty, small boys, it isn't all that complicated to differentiate them from frogs. The "giggors" are the boys.

The "giggees" are the frogs. How can you tell? By identifying the nature each possesses. Boys have human nature, frogs have frog nature. It's that simple.

Essential characteristics

There are certain *essential characteristics* common to humans; the boys have those. And there are certain essential characteristics common to frogs; the frogs have those.

Humans have a particular type of hands, feet, eyes, arms, and legs, all arranged in a consistently predictable fashion. Each one also has a soul, that is, a mind, a will, emotions, a heart, and whatever else makes up the human soul. Frogs have a distinctly different kind of "hands," feet, eyes, "arms," and legs—not to mention skin—all arranged in a predictable fashion. They have no soul.

To distinguish between frogs and boys you simply run a spot-check of their common sets of essential characteristics according to what you know about frogs and boys. That should quickly settle the question of who is what. And if there is still a doubt, that guttural "r-rrivett" is a dead giveaway of frog nature!

Now we are ready for a definition of the word *nature*. The term *nature* refers to *that set of common essential characteristics possessed by a whole group, or type, and which sets that particular group off from all other groups*—in this case boys from frogs.

Question number two is: How can we distinguish one boy from the other?

Non-essential characteristics

Nature, with its essential characteristics, refers to that which is common to a group, but it does not deal with that which distinguishes subjects within a group. For that we need to look at the *non-essential characteristics*.

Humans come with a certain common set of essential characteristics. But there is the potential for an almost infinite number of differences between humans. That's because those common essential characteristics come in an almost infinite variety of sizes, shapes, colors, and capacities—that is, non-essential characteristics.

One of the boys, let's say, is a stubby four-feet-four-inches tall, has soft brown eyes, and is average in intelligence. The other is a lanky six-feet-three-inches tall, has steel-blue eyes, and is a veritable genius. Each boy has his own "variety pack" of non-essential human characteristics. The variations in those characteristics, both of body and of soul, recognized in each "package," mark off one boy from the other. They differentiate each. The same, incidentally, is also true of the frogs and frog nature—things like size and color. We can tell frogs apart as well as humans. Each package within a kind distinguishes one from another of its kind.

Now at this point we can be satisfied with our distinctions between one frog and another. But in no way have we finished distinguishing one boy from the other, between one human being and another. We would have a limited reality if we confined all that is different between human beings to a different set of non-essential characteristics of human nature. That doesn't satisfy in explaining all that is different in us humans.

So question number three then is: Does the fact the boys have two different sets of non-essential characteristics completely establish all that is different about them? To answer that question we need to define *person.*

Person

The answer to the above question is a resounding, no. To pinpoint the uniqueness between humans we need the word *person.*

Now suppose one of our boys above has an identical twin at home. Outwardly, the two are "carbon copies." But the one twin, Johnny, loves to gig frogs while his brother, Jimmy, loathes even the thought of it, greatly preferring practicing scales on the piano. Ask the boys' mother if she has trouble telling them apart and she'll likely reply with something like, "It's easy, they're just two different persons."

Her answer is far more correct than it may seem at first. Not only do all of us have our own packages of non-essential characteristics of human nature, but *each of us also has his own unique God-made-by-special-order, God-given person.* That person literally underlies all else there is about us. It is the bottom line of who we are. Two individual humans may be ever so much alike in nature, and yet so utterly opposite in how that nature, even when packaged alike, is personally fleshed out. It is *person* that ultimately accounts for this difference and is responsible for it.

Several things can be said about this matter of person that will help bring the concept into focus.

First, both person and nature, although definitely distinct, are never separate except as abstract concepts. In flesh and blood reality, the two are necessary to form one complete, whole human being.

Second, person is God-made and God-given for each of us directly. Nature we inherit from God through our parents.

Your person is the unique creation of God for you only. There are look-alikes in non-essential characteristics, but none in person.

Third, it is your person that allows you to be a free, responsible, moral being. Nature by itself, even with its non-essential distinctives, would be subject to determinism. Person is not.

Fourth, we cannot define the full content of person. None of us knows the full content of our own person—or anyone else's. There is an element of mystery about each person.

Fifth, person is the foundational element of human uniqueness. There are many things that distinguish you from another human being. But after all other differences between, for example, our twins above are taken into account and exhausted, person is *the* bottom line. It underlies all else there is about us. We are going to have to conclude that Johnny is ultimately different from Jimmy in his "Johnnyness" as compared and contrasted to his brother's "Jimmyness." It is in knowing Johnny's "Johnnyness" and Jimmy's "Jimmyness" that person is most clearly grasped and the absolute uniqueness of these two humans is best understood.

Knowing God as Three Persons

Now that we have working definitions of person and nature, let's use them to help understand something about the Holy Trinity. Many difficulties can be cleared up using these two words.

Have you ever wondered, for example, who Jesus Christ, being God, prayed to when on the cross He prayed to God? He obviously did not pray either to Himself or to some impersonal divine nature in the sky. The answer is that as a distinct *person*, the Son, He prayed to another distinct *person*, God the Father, whose *nature* He fully shares.

The Father

God the Father is an actual, distinct person who can be known and related to personally by other persons, human as well as divine. Jesus repeatedly claimed He knew the Father (John 7:29; 8:55; Matthew 11:27). In His great prayer to the Father on the night in which He was betrayed, He made it abundantly clear that not only did He know the Father (John 17:25), but that we also can know His Father even as we can know Him. "And this is eternal life," Jesus said to His Father, "that they may know You, the only true God, and Jesus Christ whom You have sent" (John 17:3). That leaves no room for doubt. The Father and the Son are two distinct persons, and you can know them both.

When we seek understanding about the Trinity we begin with the Father. The Father is the Fountainhead of the Holy Trinity. He is not an unapproachable, vague, ethereal religious substance far removed from earth in some distant, dark recess of heaven. He is a person who is ever present, who knows and loves, and who is to be known and loved. This is apparent from Jesus' words, again on the night of the Last Supper, "If anyone loves Me, he will keep My word; and My Father will love him, and We will come to him, and make Our abode with him" (John 14:23).

Many Christians believe the Son of God lives in them personally. And many believe the Holy Spirit also personally dwells within them. It is a great wonder, but the heavenly Father also personally lives in the hearts of His people, loving them, along with His Son and His Holy Spirit. Granted that we will never in all eternity know everything about the Father. We may even come to know more about what He is by knowing what He is not. Nonetheless, we are to truly know Him.

Knowing the Father personally, as a distinct person, is all important and exceedingly desirable. And as part of coming to that knowledge, there are some profound things we can know *about* the Father. Here are just a few.

For one, the Father is eternal. He has no beginning. He has always been, He is, and He always will be (Psalm 90:2).

Second, since the Father is the source of all, all are accountable to Him. Saint Paul writes to the Ephesians, "For this reason I bow my knees to the Father . . . from whom the whole family in heaven and earth is named" (Ephesians 3:14, 15). Certainly then, all that is—whether people, angels, or whatever—all are accountable to Him as Father, and He surely has a claim on them. They are His and not their own.

Third, because the Father has an only-begotten Son after His own nature, there never was a time (or an eternity) when He was not the Father of that only-begotten Son. The Son is eternally born of Him, fully bearing the nature of His Father. "And He is the radiance of His glory and the exact representation of His nature," we read in the letter to the Hebrews (Hebrews 1:3; NASB).

(By the way, it is the relationship between God the Father and God the Son that gives us our basic understanding of human fatherhood. At the heart of the current breakdown of the family is the misbegotten attempt by some to understand fatherhood purely from a human standpoint. This failure to determine our definition of fatherhood from the divine model, the Holy Trinity, has become a major source of confusion in gender roles in our society.)

Fourth, the Father is the eternal source of the Holy Spirit, even as He is of the Son. The eternal procession of the Holy Spirit from the Father as a distinct person sharing the Father's divine nature is in a manner different from the generation of the eternal Son. That the Father is the source of the Son and the Holy Spirit does not imply there ever was a time when they did not co-exist with the Father or that they are not co-equal in all respects. The One was born of the Father before all time; the Other proceeded from the Father before all time.

The Son came to make the Father known

We must never forget that one of Jesus' objectives was to bring people to His Father as well as Himself. On the night of the Last Supper He told the disciples, "I am the way, the truth, and the life. No one comes to the Father except through Me" (John 14:6).

It is standard operating procedure in many Christian gatherings to express one's personal experience with God by saying, "I have come to know Jesus Christ personally." That is good in whatever degree it truly has happened. But strikingly, that very statement may be a tip-off betraying great spiritual poverty unless it can be said with equal conviction, "I have come to know the Father personally." If you know Jesus Christ personally you will necessarily know the Father—and the Holy Spirit—as persons. *They cannot be known apart from one another,* though one may know all three persons without being consciously aware of this necessity.

Once again, coming to know God is far more than a matter of getting an accurate knowledge of the doctrine of the Trinity. The latter must not be used as a substitute for the former. But the latter is vitally important, particularly in averting the danger of attempting to get acquainted with God as though He were some impersonal divine nature in the sky. There is no such God, and any religious experience established on that basis will be found wanting. Doctrinal knowledge cannot guarantee personal knowledge of God, but apart from such knowledge we may miss knowing that God is personal.

The Son

Of course the Son, too, is a person. Ever existing *with* the Father, He is the eternal and only-begotten Son *of* the Father. The Son possesses fully the nature of His Father. Were that not the case, He would not be a Son. In the creed we confess of the Son of God, "Begotten, not made, of one essence with the Father . . ." Essence and nature here mean the same thing.

We are so susceptible to a human perspective rather than a divine outlook that it is difficult for us to conceptualize a son co-eternal with his father. We may thoughtlessly eliminate the possibility of the Father and the Son being always co-existent because that could not be the case with us humans. But as you've noticed, humans aren't God, and there is a great difference! We need insight into what it means for the Son of God to have always co-existed with the Father.

God is uncreated and eternal. We humans are created and creatures of time. God has no beginning; we do. It is apparent that the Father, uncreated and eternal by nature, if He begets a Son, must of necessity beget an uncreated, eternal Son.

Human fathers, with their created human nature, beget human sons and daughters with created human nature, that is, their children possess the nature of their parents. Human fathers don't beget kids with bird nature or tree nature, and don't beget children with divine nature. And because we are human and bound by time, a father necessarily lives several years before He is capable of having a son. That's part of the limitation of being both created and subject to the limits of time.

But with the eternal, uncreated Father, such limitations do not exist. And thus the eternal Father necessarily begets from before all time a Son co-eternal with Himself.

The Holy Spirit

The Holy Spirit is also a person who, together with the Father and the Son, can be known personally. He is not an impersonal influence for good, as some erroneously believe. Neither is He an impersonal love which binds the Father and the Son together, as others have falsely maintained. And the Holy Spirit is not an "also ran" in the Godhead, some celestial Second Lieutenant.

The Holy Spirit is God, and like the Father and the Son, He fully and completely possesses the one undivided divine nature of the Father. He is not *begotten* of the Father; He *proceeds* from the Father. Jesus said of the Holy Spirit, "When the Helper [i.e., the Holy Spirit] comes, whom I shall send to you from the Father, the Spirit of truth who proceeds from the Father, He will testify of Me" (John 15:26). How the Holy Spirit proceeds, or comes forth, from the Father is a great mystery. But we do know it is not the same as being begotten of the Father. Both the Son and the Spirit possess the Father's nature, the Son by birth and the Holy Spirit by procession.

Jesus made it forever clear that the Holy Spirit can be known personally when He said concerning Him, "And I will pray the Father, and He will give you another Helper, that He may abide with you forever, even the Spirit of truth, whom the world cannot receive, because it neither sees Him nor *knows* Him; but you *know* Him, for He dwells with you and will be in you" (John 14:16, 17; italics mine).

That's far, far removed from the oft pompously proclaimed, "We just need to know Jesus." That is outright heresy. It denies the Bible, ignores the Creed, and blatantly denies the need for a Christian to know and experience the Holy Spirit and the Father as genuine persons.

There is a well-known and loved prayer which the Orthodox Church offers to the Holy Spirit. It expresses our constant dependence upon this divine person for His work in our lives, and it is a prayer all sincere Christians should know and use:

O Heavenly King, the Comforter, the Spirit of truth, who are in all places and fill all things, the Treasure of good things and Giver of life, come and abide in us. Cleanse us from every stain and save our souls, O Good One.

Take away the person of the Holy Spirit from your life and you've taken away the One by whom we are joined to Jesus Christ and who works out the life of Christ in us, energizing us with the power of Christ for persistent battle.

Three distinct persons—but one undivided nature

If the Father, the Son, and the Holy Spirit are three distinct, knowable persons, are there not then really three Gods? No, because even though God is three persons, there are no variety packages of non-essential characteristics of the Father's nature.

That nature is one and undivided. In our case as humans, each person has a variety package of non-essential human characteristics. There are as many of those packages as there are human beings. With God, each of the three divine persons fully and completely shares the whole of the Father's nature. This explains why every Sunday the Orthodox confess in their worship, "... the Trinity, one in essence [nature] and undivided."

Content of nature

Looking at just two aspects of nature, mind and will, can help make this sharing of one whole nature easier to understand.

Consider the question, "Does each of the three persons of the Trinity have His own mind or will distinct from the others?" The answer is categorically, no.

If each of the persons of the Trinity has a mind or will of His own, separate from the others, we would have to restate the oft asked question, "How do I know the *will* of God?" to "How do I know the *wills* of God?" Or, we would no longer inquire concerning the *mind* of God, but rather of the *minds* of God. How complicated and confusing that would be! In the multiplicity and diversity of human nature there are as many minds and wills as there are persons. But in the Trinity there is but one mind and one will shared by all three persons because all three persons share the Father's nature.

Working together in harmony

Though the Father, Son, and Holy Spirit are distinct persons, it is of the utmost importance to recognize they do not function independently of one another. They are distinct persons, and they do, as it were, some distinct things. But they *never* work separately.

Creation provides a perfect illustration of how the Holy Three work together in perfect harmony. We read in Genesis 1:26 that God said, "Let *Us* make man in *Our* image, according to *Our* likeness . . ." (italics mine). Who made people? The Father did; the Son did; the Holy Spirit did. God did. But that is not to imply the Father, Son, and Holy Spirit each did exactly the same thing in the creation of humanity. Each had a role, yet together they created our race. The Scriptures say of the Son, "All things were made through Him, and without Him nothing was made that was made" (John 1:3), and of the Spirit, ". . . and the Spirit of God was hovering over the face of the waters" (Genesis 1:2).

Gathering together several of the Scriptural texts on this subject, a kind of pattern surfaces showing how the Father, the Son, and the Holy Spirit work as one. That is: *from* the Father, *through* the Son, and *in* the Holy Spirit. Three in one. Unity.

I remember reading some years ago the work of a rather well-known theologian who insisted the Father alone was responsible for creation, the Son alone was responsible for procuring our redemption, and the Holy Spirit alone was responsible for working our salvation in us. It was as if each person of the Godhead had His own private area of responsibility, to the exclusion of that of the others. Unionized perhaps! That kind of fuzzy thinking not only confuses people immeasurably in regard to the Trinity, but it prevents them from knowing those persons in their experience.

Knowing persons as persons

Let me illustrate this matter of knowing God personally by considering a seriously endangered aspect of human experience—marriage. Imagine a young man and young woman who meet and are greatly attracted to each other. He is attracted by her beautiful face, flowing blonde hair, curvaceous body, and brilliant mind. She is attracted to his muscular physique, his curly, thick brown hair, an ever-present twinkle in his eyes, and his lightning-quick wit. They assume this mutual attraction to each other is love and marry.

Three children and twenty years later her face is lined, her hair graying, the curves in her body have significantly shifted. And his once muscular body has given way to a body with no definition except the very noticeable one around the middle. The curly, thick brown hair is no more—most of it having been exchanged for a shiny, bony, bald head with just a wisp of grey hair around the edges. His eyes are tired now from the pressures of worry and care, and the quick wit is replaced by a steady diet of biting sarcasm.

One day our once-young man sees a young woman with a beautiful face, flowing blond hair, curvaceous body, and a brilliant mind. He becomes increasingly attracted to her and at the same time progressively disenchanted with his wife of twenty years, the mother of his children. Somewhat bewildered by what he views as a change of attractions, he's trying to figure out how to dispose of an "old" love to give himself to this "new" love for which he finds himself so passionately burning.

An unreal scenario? It's happening all around us every day, leaving a path of devastated people and relationships in its wake.

What happened?

One answer may well be that our original couple never really got to know each other as *persons*. What they mistook for love was limited to mutual attraction to an appealing "variety pack" of non-essential characteristics of human nature. As those "packages" aged, sagged, rearranged, and faded, they lost their appeal. And as soon as an attraction to another "package" developed, interest was lost in the old, with all the attention going to the new.

Solid marriage relationships demand people know each other as utterly unrepeatable, unique persons. Sure the variety packages are there, and they aren't unimportant. But lacking knowledge of each other as persons, and building a relationship mostly between different variety packs, is not a sound basis for a personal relationship, something which marriage needs to possess.

As in our relationships with people, so in our relationship with God. He must be known personally to really be known at all. Many have had an attraction to or an awareness of God in their youth. But their knowledge of God never passed beyond an initial excitement about learning a set of divine attributes, that He is infinite, eternal, unchangeable—even love. But to truly know God is to know Him as Father, Son, and Holy Spirit; in that knowledge, there is great and lasting fulfillment.

Is it necessary to understand this discussion for you to be a Christian? Or to have faith in God? I have neither said nor implied such a thing. But faith does rest on the solid rock of reality, and this includes a God who is three persons, and who can be known as such. It is in Him we are called upon to have faith.

The Christian life is not "just knowing Jesus." To reduce things down that far cuts spiritual living into spiritual ribbons. And when it comes to the heat of spiritual conflict, no victory can begin apart from knowing God personally. There's more to be done for victory than that, but apart from knowing God, personal conflict will always end in defeat.

Chapter Five

THE WORD BECAME FLESH

Tell us, O Joseph, how is it that you brought the Virgin whom you received . . . to Bethlehem great with child? And he replies, saying, I have searched the Prophets, and it was revealed to me by the angel. Therefore, I am convinced that Mary shall give birth in an inexplicable manner to God, whom Magi from the east shall come to worship and to service with precious gifts. Wherefore, O You who was incarnate for our sakes, glory to You.—An Orthodox Nativity Hymn

The coming in the flesh of the eternal Son of the Father, the second person of the Holy Trinity, is the greatest event in the history of the human race. Angels celebrated His birth by singing, "Glory to God in the highest." And in reflecting upon His becoming man, men and women in the Church of old cried, "O Great mystery." Twenty centuries later we still stand amazed at this mystery of the incarnation.

Marvel of marvels, God the Son was born as a human being. He took human nature to Himself as His very own. Incarnation literally means "infleshment." It was the incarnation the Apostle John was describing when he wrote, "And the Word became flesh and dwelt among us, and we beheld His glory, the glory as of the only begotten of the Father, full of grace and truth" (John 1:14). The Word of God, that is, God the Son, became a man. He became incarnate. He became flesh. The three statements are synonymous.

Nothing could be more important for us to grasp than this mystery. It was He who "... for us men and for our salvation came down from heaven and was made flesh by the Holy Spirit and the Virgin Mary, and became man..." Our salvation depends upon the incarnation more than our life depends on breath. We cannot afford to be ignorant of this great mystery. Forget the thought that the incarnation is "too theological" to understand. Do not buy the deceptive rhetorical boast that all we need do is just believe in the "simple Jesus." We can't comprehend all that is involved in the Son of God taking on human flesh, but it is imperative we know the reality of the incarnation and the identity of the One incarnate. We can be Christian without a full grasp of this truth. But to "fight the good fight of faith" we need clear understanding on this issue.

Something Assumed: A "Package" of Human Nature

The Son of God, in addition to the divine nature He possessed from the Father from all eternity, took to Himself a "package," as it were, of human nature in the womb of the Virgin Mary.

This is critically important: He did not dispose of or set

aside His divine nature, not even temporarily. Rather, He assumed to Himself another nature, a human nature, which was conceived in Mary and assumed by Him in the very same instant. A perfect union of two natures, one divine and the other human, was accomplished in the person of the Son of God. The theologians call this the 'hypostatic union.'

He did not take to Himself a human person. He was one divine person, the Son, but now with two distinct natures united in that one person. So the Son became a man without for an instant ceasing to be fully God. He always was, is, and ever will be truly God. But He is also, since His 'infleshment,' truly man, and will be forever.

Keep in mind here, we're talking about one person with two natures, and thus we have *one* Son, but in *two* natures. Had He assumed a human person, as well as a human nature, we would have two Sons with no actual union between them. One person would be divine; the other would be human. Had that been the case, there would have been no real incarnation. Instead of the Son of God Himself coming in the flesh, we would have had the formation of a new creature also called the Son of God, but in the human aspect that title would have been in name only. Such a second Son could only be called the Son of God by His association, as it were, with the Son of God, but He could not truly be called God.

Further, had there been two persons and two natures in Christ there would be no hope for fallen humanity whatsoever, because neither Son could save us. The one Son could not save because He would not be divine, and it takes God to save man. The other could not save because, not being born of fallen humanity, He would not be joining this race of ours to God, bringing us into union with Him.

The "two person" or "two Son" idea, to identify Christ, has come up from time to time in the history of the Church. Always it has been shown to be false and rejected as such. Such a "Jesus" would be useless.

It all Began in the Womb of Mary

How, when, and where did this wonder of the incarnation take place? In the womb of the Virgin Mary. This uniting of human nature to the Son of God took place not at His birth but at His conception in her womb.

Obviously, Mary wasn't responsible for the origin of the person of her Son or of His divine nature. That would make her God, and she is not. She wasn't even responsible for her own pregnancy, although she wholeheartedly consented to it when she said, "Behold the maidservant of the Lord! Let it be to me according to your word" (Luke 1:38). The Holy Spirit was responsible for that miraculous conception. Yet it was from Mary that the Son received His human nature. For His human mind, His human body, His human soul, His human will all came from her. In His humanity, He, like Mary, was one of us.

Because Jesus was indeed the son of Mary, we also unequivocally reject the error of thinking the Son of God just "adopted" that human nature for some thirty-three years, only to put it aside when He returned to heaven. That is not so. The human nature the Son of God assumed from Mary was, and still is, as fully His by birth as your nature is to you.

Mary, the Mother of God

The incarnation of Christ makes Mary the mother of the Son of God in His humanity. God the Son actually experienced human conception in her and human birth from her. Upon conception He came to dwell in her womb, taking His humanity from her. She didn't give birth to some non-personal nature. She bore a real, true child. Her child was God in the flesh. She is thus "Holy Mary, Mother of God."

Many people are being tragically robbed of the marvelous reality of Mary being the mother of God because they assume that means she gave deity to her Son. She wasn't the origin of His divine person or His divine nature, but she was the mother of God the Son, whom she bore in her womb. If Mary was not the mother of God, the bearer of the second person of the Trinity, then the baby she brought into this world was merely a man, and we are all, no matter how much we believe in Him, still in our sins and "having no hope and without God in the world" (Ephesians 2:12). If it was not God who was in her womb our only hope is death. Thus it is to honor Christ Himself, that we boldly call the one who bore Him, "Mother of God."

The Father and the Holy Spirit did not Become Incarnate

What about the Father and the Holy Spirit? Did they too become man? Absolutely not. Though all three divine persons were active together in the Son's becoming a man, only the Son assumed human nature. The Father *sent* the Son (I John 4:14), and the Holy Spirit was responsible for His conception in Mary (Matthew 1:20), but it was only the Son who assumed human flesh.

The Father and the Holy Spirit were, however, continually and intimately related to the Son during His sojourn on earth. They were always with Him in all He did. Of His relationship to the Father, Jesus said, "Do you not believe that I am in the Father, and the Father in Me? . . . the Father who dwells in Me does the works" (John 14:10).

The Holy Spirit was with Him too. When Jesus came up from the water after being baptized by John in the Jordan, the Holy Spirit descended upon Him and *remained* (John 1:33), even as the Father spoke. There is no way the divine persons can possibly have a more constant and intimate relationship than that.

A Landmark in Church History

For the better part of four centuries (A.D. 300 - A.D. 700), there was continual inquiry and debate in the Christian Church on the subject of the incarnation and different aspects of it. During the fifth century in particular, some Christian teachers were claiming Jesus Christ was two persons with two natures. (Remember, that would make two Sons of God.) These claims were in contrast to others who erroneously taught that He was one person, but with two natures that had blended, co-mingled, into one nature. They failed to realize such a person could be neither divine nor human, and that this blend would leave Christ neither God nor man. This latter teaching is called "monophysitism." Both arguments were heresies. Both needed correction.

The heated and occasionally even violent controversy on these issues peaked in A.D. 451 at Chalcedon (also a city only a few miles from present day Istanbul) where bishops, elders, and deacons came from throughout the ancient world to meet for what is now referred to as the Fourth Ecumenical Council, the Council of Chalcedon. Their task was to set forth what had always been believed about Jesus Christ's deity and humanity.

The deliberations went on for weeks. This could not be done quickly or carelessly. Finally, the following creed was presented. You will benefit by reading it slowly and carefully.

Therefore, following the holy Fathers, we all with one accord teach men to acknowledge one and the same Son, our Lord Jesus Christ, at once complete in Godhead and complete in manhood, truly God and truly man, consisting also of a reasonable soul and body; of one substance with the Father as regards His Godhead, and at the same time of one substance with us as regards His manhood; like us in all respects, apart from sin; as regards His Godhead, begotten of the Father before the ages, but yet as regards His manhood begotten, for us men and for our salvation, of Mary the virgin, the God-bearer; one and the same Christ, Son, Lord, Only-begotten, recognized in two natures, without confusion, without change, without division, without separation; the distinction of natures being in no way annulled by the union, but rather the characteristics of each nature being preserved and coming together to form one person and subsistence, not as parted or separated into two persons, but one and the same Son and Only-begotten God the Word, Lord Jesus Christ; even as the prophets from earliest times spoke of Him, and our Lord Jesus Christ Himself taught us, and the creed of the Fathers has handed down to us.

There is a report that when this statement was read, the bishops proclaimed with one voice, "This is the faith of the

Fathers; this is the doctrine of the Apostles!" Since then that statement has been the standard of truth on this subject for all Christians, whether they be Protestant, Roman Catholic, Anglican, or Orthodox.

Jesus Christ "Used" both Natures

One critical point expressed in the creed is: ". . . in two natures without *confusion*, without *change*, without *division*, without *separation;* the distinction of natures being in no way annulled by the union . . ." One thing this means is that throughout Jesus' life and ministry He constantly expressed Himself in both natures at the same time. He thought, willed, and loved through both His human nature and His divine nature at once.

Call to mind the time Jesus healed a man who had been born blind. Jesus spat on the ground, made mud with the saliva, daubed it on the man's sightless eyes, and told him to go wash in the pool of Siloam. The man did as Jesus instructed him, and miraculously received his sight.

Did Jesus do that as God or as a man? Because Christ is one person, He cannot be divided that way. The one person acts in both natures in whatever way is appropriate to each. The One who is the Creator of human eyes was the One who was the healer of human eyes that day. Human saliva was daubed on by human hands. Nonetheless it was done by the eternal Son of God, now also a man. He acted in both natures.

Then there was the time Jesus walked on the water. With that miracle in mind, think about what the Apostle Paul says about Christ, "For by Him all things were created that are in heaven and that are on earth, visible and invisible, whether thrones or dominions or principalities or powers. All things were created through Him and for Him. And He is before all things, and in Him all things consist" (Colossians 1:16, 17). What happened that day when He walked on water? The very Creator of water, and the One at that very moment holding that water together, God the Son, walked on that water with human feet, saw the waves with human eyes, and reached out with human hands to help the faltering Peter.

There are Christians who believe that Christ performed all His miracles in His human nature only, and that His divine nature was passive during His entire sojourn on earth. This would demand that God do something He cannot do. God does not, and cannot, stop being and behaving as God, even when He becomes a man.

The One who with the Father and the Holy Spirit was the Creator and Sustainer of the universe was not the ex-Creator and ex-Sustainer of the water the day He walked on the water. Nor was He the off-duty Creator and Sustainer of men the day He healed the blind man's eyes. He was the Creator and Sustainer who had become man by uniting to Himself human nature in the womb of the Virgin Mary.

He must not be viewed as being sometimes God and sometimes man. From His conception on He has been both, and He forever will be. This may not seem significant here, but it will be crucial when we consider Jesus' crucifixion and resurrection from the dead.

He Emptied Himself

The awesome condescension of the Son of the Father in becoming a man is summed up in Philippians, where Paul, speaking of Him, said: "Who, although He existed in the form [form here means nature] of God, did not regard equality with

God a thing to be grasped, but emptied Himself, taking the form of a bond-servant, and being made in the likeness of men" (Philippians 2:6, 7; NASB). That phrase, "emptied Himself," refers to the fact that the eternal Son of God willingly subjected His divine person to the limitations of human nature as He expressed Himself in His humanity. It means that the eternal Son of the Father subjected Himself to a common human birth, and that as a baby He messed His diapers (or whatever they used) and He was fed at Mary's breast.

It means also that in His flesh the Son of God increased in wisdom and stature with God and men. He experienced hunger and sorrow—as well as human joy and satisfaction. He experienced pain if He hit His finger with a hammer in Joseph's carpenter shop. He experienced genuine temptation. The eternal Son of God in His humanity had to be fully and completely all that we are, except that He was without sin.

Most of All

Still more is involved in the words, "emptied Himself." First, for us humans so greatly in need of a Savior, it is important beyond description that we firmly understand that the very person of the Son of God subjected Himself to a human death in His own flesh. That's emptying!

He did not, and could not, suffer in His divine nature. Divine nature can neither suffer nor die. But in His flesh, in His human nature, the Son of God experienced all the trauma, all the excruciating pain, every trace of suffering that a human can experience in such a death as His. The very One who in His divine nature was holding together the wood of the cross on which He was being crucified, and the iron of the nails they drove into His hands and feet, the One responsible for wood and iron even being in existence, was the same person who felt the burning sting of those nails as He hung on that wooden cross. The suffering of the Son of God on the cross was no mere "apparent" suffering. It was stark reality in all of its true horror for the Son of God. "He emptied Himself."

Second, He became sin for us. The creed of Chalcedon confesses, "He was made like us in all respects, apart from sin." Yet, He who was without sin for the more than 17,500,000 minutes of His earthly life, bore our sins in His own body on the cross. Paul said of Christ, "He [the Father] made Him [Christ] who knew no sin to be sin for us, that we might become the righteousness of God in Him" (II Corinthians 5:21). And, speaking prophetically of the Son of God, Isaiah had said, ". . . the Lord has laid on Him the iniquity of us all" (Isaiah 53:6).

The perfect Son of God became the sacrifice for our sins. Every time the bread for Communion is prepared in our Church the following words are said, "You, O Savior, have bought us from the curse of the Law by Your precious blood. . . . The Lamb of God, Who takes away the sin of the world, is sacrificed for the life and salvation of the world."

When I was in seminary I recall asking over and over again a question that had bothered me for years: "Who was it, really, who died on the cross?"

Of course I knew the answer I would get: "It was Jesus Christ."

I knew that. What I wanted to know was: Did God die? If Jesus Christ is both God and man, did God die, or was it just a man?

I discussed the question with fellow students and professors, but I could never get a crisp answer. Even the teachers I asked didn't appear sure. The question lingered in my mind, and it would be many years before I was sure of the answer: God the Son died in His flesh.

The Lord Jesus Christ, the One who was begotten of the Father before all time, and who assumed human nature, died in His humanity for us and for our salvation. And while divine nature cannot itself die, nonetheless the very person of the Son became a sacrifice for our sins. Little wonder, then, that Charles Wesley, the Methodist hymn writer, took up his pen to write:

Amazing love, how can it be
That Thou, my God, shouldst die for me!

Just as surely as the baby Mary bore was the Son of God in His flesh, so every bit as surely the One she watched die at Calvary was the same Son of God.

There is More than Forgiveness

The death of the eternal Son of the Father in His flesh is the basis for the forgiveness of our sins. But if forgiveness were the sum-total of our salvation, there would still be no help for us in our striving against sin. Salvation is much more than forgiveness. The Son of God did not stay dead. He rose from the dead. There is, therefore, necessarily a new life for the forgiven to live—a life based on His resurrection. This life is as dependent on the Son of God becoming a man as is forgiveness of sins.

In fact, it's because of the matter of this new life and how it affects our war with sin that I took so much time on all this data about Jesus being one person with two natures. You see, it is God's design that a living union be established between the Forgiver and the forgiven so that the forgiven can now live like the Forgiver. In that union we are empowered, energized, to do His will. An understanding of exactly what that means and how it works can be helped greatly by considering the distinctiveness of the two natures of Jesus Christ and how they relate in His one person. So let us focus in on that again.

The Relationship of the Two Natures

"In two natures without *confusion*, without *change*, without *division*, and without *separation*." That's an exceptionally tightly worded statement. Those four words in the Creed of Chalcedon have served as the guide to all Christians since to understand and describe what the Scriptures teach about the relationship between the two natures of Jesus Christ.

His divine nature and His human nature are united inseparably in the one person. Yet there is no mingling, or confusion, of those two natures. Each nature retains its own distinctiveness. Should the divine nature and the human nature of Jesus Christ be mingled together—be blended or homogenized—so as to lose their distinctiveness, the result would be some hybrid nature which was neither divine nor human.

The idea that the natures are mingled has often been proposed, and that explanation has just as often been rejected by the Church because it is untrue and such a belief is disastrous to our salvation. Don't forget, the divine nature of the Son is the exact same nature the Father and the Holy Spirit possess. If the divine nature of the Son could be altered by mixing human nature into it, the whole Godhead would be affected the same way, because the Father, the Son, and the

Holy Spirit fully possess the same divine nature. Alter the divine nature in any one of the three divine persons and the divine nature is altered in all three. "The Trinity, one in essence and undivided" would cease being God and necessarily become a blending of God and man. The resulting God-man mixture would be a pathetic, mythical creature unable to be either God or man. The God of the universe would no longer exist.

This "blending" teaching finds itself quite at home in some Eastern religions and in various modern so-called Christian cults, but it has no place whatsoever in the historic Orthodox faith.

One Nature Interpenetrates the Other

However, though there is no confusion or blending of the two natures of Christ, those two natures do not merely exist side by side in the one person with no effect of one on the other. There is a true union of the natures in the one person. Get a glimpse of how these two natures are related in Christ, and we can begin to fathom how the Christian is impacted by his or her relationship to Jesus Christ.

The sword in the fire

To understand the relationship Christ's two natures have to each other, consider an illustration used often throughout the history of the Church. (It will be referred to several more times in this book.) Imagine a steel sword being heated in a fire. The sword becomes red hot. Does the sword become blended with the fire so that the fire and sword become one substance? Obviously not. The sword is still distinctly steel and the fire is still distinctly fire. The steel does not become fire, nor does the fire become steel. But the sword does get hot. It *partakes* of the heat of the fire. The heat of fire, the energy of the fire, interpenetrates the substance of the sword.

This time-proven illustration is helpful in our understanding the relationship between Christ's two natures, and in particular the effect of Christ's divine nature on His human nature. As the energy of the fire interpenetrates the sword and in so doing heats it, so the divine nature of Christ interpenetrates His human nature with the divine energies—such as wisdom, love, and holiness.

We can say without hesitation that the humanity of Christ was *divinized.* Human nature was transformed, renewed, in Christ. The purpose of God for humanity is completely fulfilled in Christ. Deity transformed humanity by energizing it in the union of those two natures in the One person of Christ. Chapter eight is devoted to covering this subject in more detail, and applying it to our salvation.

The energies of Christ's divine nature immeasurably affect and influence His human nature. All that Jesus was, said, and did in His earthly ministry was affected by that interpenetration. That's one reason He could say, "He who has seen Me has seen the Father . . ." (John 14:9).

Two Natures Always Working Together

In chapter four, I pointed out that because there is only one divine nature there is only one will and mind for the Father, Son, and Holy Spirit. But the Son, after He became a man, and thus having a human soul, has two minds and two wills. He has a divine mind and will, and He also has a human mind and will.

The fact that Jesus has a divine will and a human will is an important aid to our understanding of what was happening when Jesus, knowing He was about to be crucified, was praying in the Garden of Gethsemane! Here was a real human drama. It is not natural for any human being to desire to suffer in dying. Jesus was no exception. Suffering, however, happened to be the will of God in His case. Whatever protests His humanity might genuinely offer, He could still say, "O My Father, if it is possible, let this cup pass from Me; nevertheless, not as I will, but as You will" (Matthew 26:39).

There was (and still is) in Jesus Christ a constant working together of His two natures in their totality. This working together of Christ's two natures was vitally necessary to the accomplishment of His whole ministry. Jesus could say, "For I have come down from heaven, not to do My own will, but the will of Him who sent Me" (John 6:38). He had two wills. But His human will was perfectly submitted to the divine will. The one person voluntarily willed the same thing in both natures.

Resurrection and Ascension

After He died on the cross, Jesus Christ did not cease possessing two natures. His human nature did not remain in the grave when He rose from the dead. If it had, humanity itself would have remained without hope. He died as a man, and He also was raised from the dead in His own humanity.

This same One also ascended into heaven in His humanity and took His seat at the right hand of the Father. He had left that throne to become the Son of Man, to unite to Himself human nature. He returned to His Father's throne with that humanity. In the fullest sense of the word, there is right now a *Man* who has been crowned Lord of all seated at the very throne of God in heaven.

Not just an action of God for a span of thirty-three years, the incarnation of the Son of God is for all eternity. The Savior and King, Jesus Christ, is still fully God and fully man, one person, "...in two natures without confusion, without change, without division, and without separation." Why the infinite and glorious second person of the most Holy and Blessed Trinity should so humble Himself for all eternity is beyond our imagining. Yet it is so. His love knows no limits. We can surely agree, "To Him belongs glory, honor, and worship now and ever, and unto ages of ages. Amen."

At the very least, all this means mercy, life, peace, salvation and visitation, and pardon and remission of our sins and transgressions—plus, who knows how much more? And for our purposes here, it is the foundation for our war against sin.

Chapter Six

I BELIEVE IN THE REMISSION OF SINS

O Most Holy Trinity, have mercy on us. O Lord, cleanse us from our sins. O Master, pardon our iniquities. O Holy One, visit and heal our infirmities, for Your Name's sake.
—*An Orthodox prayer to the Trinity*

Then there are those times in your battle with sin that your behavior falls particularly short of your bare-minimum expectations. I have grim memories of one of the worst for me.

It was some years ago now, and my business partner and I had almost finished painting a severely dilapidated commercial building in downtown Santa Barbara, California. Short of a total remodel, there was no earthly way that rickety structure with its dry-rot and pealing paint could ever have been made to look good, but we had worked exceptionally hard and done our best.

About mid-morning the owner came by to inspect our progress. His expectations disappointed, he commenced to complain at great length about our work. Not only did he not appreciate our extra effort, he was demanding additional work from us that was totally unreasonable and far beyond the terms of the contract.

I listened impatiently to his fault-finding for about ten or fifteen minutes, building up internal steam steadily. Then came the explosion. I reciprocated by berating him in every manner I could think of. I could be heard for I don't know how far. Totally out of control, I had given in to the passion of anger.

My outburst occurred about 11:00 a.m., and I spent the hour before lunch nursing that familiar, empty, sick feeling you get in the pit of your stomach when you've really blown it. No one needed to inform me I'd sinned. And it was academic whether the owner was right or wrong; I had completely lost my temper. I was wrong. I had offended both God and man.

At lunch, my partner, who hadn't yet commented about the incident, looked across the table at me and said, "I guess we get worse as we get older." He wasn't trying to be ornery. In his roundabout way he was attempting to console me because he knew I was discouraged.

The overwhelming sense of self-condemnation after such an outburst can be devastating. I felt accused and defeated. "So you're a Christian? So you think you want to know God and have a personal relationship with Him? Get serious! There's no way someone who does the things you do could really be much of a Christian." Those kinds of things came to my mind.

Though defeated, guilty, and discouraged, you don't give up on the faith in such a situation. But you sure don't want a repeat performance.

So how do you proceed?

You turn to God for forgiveness, and then seek His grace

to overcome.

This chapter is about forgiveness and how to receive it—about what God has done in Christ to remove our sins from us "as far as the east is from the west," as the Scriptures say (Psalm 103:12). An understanding of forgiveness is worth all the effort necessary to grasp it, for without that understanding there is no possibility of progress in our capacity to resist sin successfully.

Forgiven, Not Excused

My blow-up that day was sin—sin against the owner of the building, sin against my partner, sin against all who could hear me, sin against myself, and, of course, it was a sin against God. I started making excuses. You know, "the owner was a jerk," and the whole stream of thought that follows. But excuses for sins won't do. We may have a thousand and one plausible explanations for our sinful acts, but none of them has any effect in remitting even one of our sins or changing our conduct the least bit.

God doesn't excuse our sins either. He forgives them. Indeed, in Christ He has done all that is necessary for our forgiveness. But there are some things we must do in order to receive forgiveness. It is not automatic. Four concrete actions are necessary if we are to know and experience God's forgiveness for our sins: *repentance, confession, faith,* and *obedience.* God supplies the grace for us to perform all of these, but we must willingly choose to avail ourselves of that grace and respond with the actions He calls for.

Repentance

For many of us, repentance may need to begin with a

change in our attitude toward sinning. If you believe it is inevitable you commit certain sins, and that you're "dead in the water" by default as soon as a specific temptation comes, you need to change your mind about that. It's possible you were taught that it is just natural to sin. That is not true. Sin is not natural. It is not only against God, it is against our nature. The Holy Scriptures, which enjoin us over and over not to sin, assume sin is unnatural.

Believing certain sins are inevitable virtually rules out your true repentance from those sins. How can we be genuinely repentant for doing what we can't help doing? Besides, what good would it do to repent if you are going to do it again the next time that same temptation comes around?

Having changed our minds about the inevitability of certain sins, next we need to set our hearts not to sin. The assumption that we're destined to commit at least certain particularly besetting sins is often accompanied by the corollary supposition, "Well, God forgives. I won't even try to resist this temptation." That kind of presumption hardens the heart and suppresses faith.

The matter of the set of the heart becomes more important when we realize our sins have consequences in our lives, and usually in the lives of others. Sin is not merely the violation of a law, for example going fifty miles-per-hour in a thirty mile-per-hour zone. In that situation, assuming you're caught, you pay a fine, and it's all over. End of consequences. If you don't get a ticket, there may be no consequences at all for your infraction. But it's not that way with sin.

In terms of consequences, God's moral and spiritual laws are akin to His natural laws, such as the law of gravity. Jump off a twenty-story building and you get mashed when you hit bottom. You don't avoid the consequences because there is no cosmic cop to see you jumping and give you a ticket. You're caught by the consequences every time because you hit bottom. No exceptions. It's a law. That's how it is with sin. "You shall not commit adultery" is an example. This is no arbitrary prohibition dreamed up by the Holy Trinity to prevent humans from having fun. Adultery has serious consequences—always!—just as surely as jumping from a twenty-story building. Adultery will always affect the offender's relationship with God negatively. It will adversely affect him personally. It cripples marriages and traumatizes children—including those not yet born. It even does damage to the society in which we live. Adultery is a violation of human nature, and it is because of its grave consequences God said, "Don't do it." Adultery is sex without true love. That is contrary to human nature as God created it. Both because of the sin itself and its repercussions we need to set our hearts not to sin.

Having rejected the inevitability of sin, and set our hearts not to sin, we then need to repent anytime we sin—and *as often as* we sin. Repentance is the first word of the gospel. As He began His public ministry, Jesus said, "Repent, for the Kingdom of God is at hand" (Matthew 4:17). Apart from repentance there is no forgiveness of sins.

At least three things are involved in sincere repentance.

1) We must agree with God that what we did was sin. We don't argue with God over the content of sin. Besides, the only thing God forgives is sin, so the sooner we agree with Him about what we've done, the sooner we're able to receive His forgiveness.

2) Our agreement with God must be accompanied by

godly sorrow (II Corinthians 7:10) for committing the sin. Godly sorrow for sin penetrates to the depths of the human heart. It is sorrow for the offense to God and heart-felt grief over the consequences in both the life of the one who committed the sin and those whom the sin affects. It is sorrow for falling short of the mark God has set, for failing to do God's will. This is the sorrow that leads to repentance and works repentance. One of the great illustrations of godly sorrow for sin is the Apostle Peter after his three-fold denial of the Lord. The Scriptures report that afterwards, "Peter went out and wept bitterly" (Luke 22:62).

3) We must turn from our sin, seeking God's grace not to do it again. You resolve you are going to be different, to live differently—no matter how difficult, no matter how many times you've got to get up and go again after a fall. This change cannot be accomplished without the power of God working in you. But change will not take place without your will being totally set to make the change.

Finally, repentance is not a one-time affair. That's not even a possibility. Repentance is a life-long practice. It may begin in a moment, and we may truly turn to God in that moment. What needs to happen in that moment is to begin a process in which a purification of the mind and the struggle against sinful thoughts progresses. True repentance is a rooting out of sin, and that is not completed in the spontaneity of a moment.

Only in relatively recent years has the spiritually suicidal heresy that repentance is a one-time affair become widely held in some Christian circles. Spiritual growth stops with the cessation of repentance, and spiritual lethargy sets in. How often do we need to repent? As often as we sin! Jesus said,

"Repent and believe in the gospel" (Mark 1:15). Repentance is no more a one-time event, never to be repeated, than is belief. When we cease believing, we must return again to belief; and when we sin again, we must repent once more.

In summary, repentance is a change of mind about sin. It is being sincerely sorry for falling short of the mark God has set. It is turning from that sin with all your heart. And it's not one time, it's lifetime. You cannot achieve repentance in your own strength, but by the empowering grace of God you can, if you will. It is the first condition for forgiveness.

Confession

Action number two leading to forgiveness is confession of sin. Confession is not an option for anyone who desires to be forgiven. To confess your sins means to acknowledge them to God. You name them.

Confession of sin needs to be practiced from two perspectives. The first is confession made directly to God. Daily in our prayers we should confess to God the sins we are aware of and ask Him to cover those we are not aware of. Confession of this kind should be a well-formed habit in our lives as Christians. The fifty-first Psalm is a powerful aid in confession of this kind.

The second perspective is the confession of sin which Orthodox Christians call the sacrament (or mystery) of repentance. This sacrament requires confession to God in the presence of a priest. Roman Catholics, Protestants, Orthodox—all Christians—need this dimension of confession. It is especially important: 1) to experience freedom from the guilt of more serious sins, 2) to bring a sin to its conclusion, 3) to terminate many or most of sin's damaging consequences, and

I BELIEVE IN THE REMISSION OF SINS

4) to break the tyranny of a passion, a besetting sin. The power of some sins will never be broken without it.

Regrettably, there are those who say, "I confess only to God Himself." Many so convinced are totally sincere, but are unfortunately trapped by the harsh realities of history, particularly history since the Protestant Reformation. There is ambivalence and confusion over this issue of confession.

Confession was practiced in New Testament times (James 5:16; Acts 19:18; I John 1:9), and that practice has continued unbroken since in the Orthodox Church. There is value in confession one to another and prayer for one another. God answers others' prayers regarding your sins.

I once thought, and I know multitudes who still do, that going to confession was a joke, or an evil thing, perhaps invented by the devil. We often ridiculed Catholic friends going to confession, and even pitied them. Mine was a quite emotionally charged reaction, anchored in some gross abuses at the time of the Reformation. The baby was thrown out with the bath-water.

The abuse of something good is rarely a reason for rejecting it. Many, I believe, reject altogether the practice of confession because of past abuses—and there were abuses. I have yet to hear, however, of any of our old crowd calling, say, for an abstinence from sex because of the many serious abuses of sex. Logic gets distorted when mingled with emotion, does it not? Wisdom must prevent us from allowing someone else's bad history to lead us to watered-down, unbiblical theology.

Further, confessing before a godly pastor is good psychology. In fact, the case can be made that modern psychologists have replaced parish priests. God made us in such a way that

85

this kind of confession is solid mental health—as well as solid spiritual health. Confession in this context is the foundation of effective pastoral counseling.

Unfortunately for those who reject confession in the presence of a priest, there are some sins which never are brought to the light in any other way. The pattern or cycle of sin goes on unbroken. Some who refuse confession in the presence of a priest, insisting they privately confess their sins to God, actually coddle serious sins with no intention of changing their way in regard to the sin. And some, even after true repentance has taken place, without the "concluding" action of confession, never completely resolve their feelings of guilt.

Others are too ashamed to confess their sins to God in the presence of their priest or pastor. It might be well to ask, how can I in sincerity confess before the Holy, Almighty God, if I can't admit these sins before sinners like myself?

And let me assure you, a priest can't forgive sins. Only God can do that, but He has included the priesthood as a part of that process. The Orthodox priest says to those who come to confess their sins in the sacrament of repentance, "My spiritual child, who has confessed to my humble person, I, humble and sinner, have not power on earth to forgive sins, but God alone; but through that divinely spoken word which came to the Apostles after the resurrection of our Lord Jesus Christ, saying: Whosever sins you remit, they are remitted, and whosoever sins you retain, they are retained, we also with boldness dare to say: Whatsoever you have said to my humble person, and whatsoever you have failed to say, whether through ignorance or forgetfulness, whatever it may be, may God forgive you in this present world, and in that which is to come."

And God does forgive. You can be sure of it. The priest will often add, "And now, having no further care for the sins you have confessed, go in peace." That's assurance! That's the fruit of confession.

One further benefit of confession is the possibility of developing a relationship with a spiritual father or spiritual guide. There is a great degree of arrogance in attempting to progress spiritually on our own. Scripture knows little of this—perhaps John the Baptist was an exception and perhaps Paul. But they are exceptions. Confession to a priest may be the beginning of such a relationship.

Christian people labor, trying their best to conquer a besetting sin, but they fail because they lack God's provision for confession. You who are not Orthodox, who sincerely desire to deal with your sins but have no priest, go to a godly pastor whom you can trust with a confidence. Confess before God in his presence. You will gain much benefit in your battle with sin.

Confession is our preamble to forgiveness. You need both the daily habit of confession to God and the regular habit of confession to God in the sacrament of repentance.

Faith

Action number three required for forgiveness is faith. Repentance and confession, if they are to bear the fruit of forgiveness, must be accompanied by faith. Faith is far more than mere mental assent to a body of religious data. Faith is dynamic, the living action of the soul trusting fully in God. And faith must be a current reality, not the memory of an experience in the past.

Two fundamental questions about faith must be answered: What is the *source* of faith? What is the *content* of faith?

The source of faith

Faith calls us to rely wholly upon what God has revealed to the eyes of the heart. But though you must do the believing, you are in no way the source of your faith. Christ is the source. He gives the grace to believe, for faith is a gift of God (Ephesians 2:8, 9). Then, in response, you receive the gift to believe. There is a necessary working together with Christ in this.

In a very real sense your faith is His faith. Saint Paul testified to the Galatians, "The life which I now live in the flesh I live by faith in the Son of God, who loved me and gave Himself for me" (Galatians 2:20). "Faith in the Son of God" should be translated "the faith of the Son of God." The faith is Christ's. He willingly gives it. You willingly receive it and exercise it.

The content of faith

God-given faith has content. Faith as a vague concept—as in, "it's important for me to believe in something greater than myself"—is useless. Honest-to-goodness faith believes what is right and true. To begin with, it believes what God Himself has done for us in the incarnation, death, and resurrection of Jesus Christ. At least three aspects of what God has done in Christ need to be assimilated into the content of faith.

1) Jesus Christ is our sacrifice for sin.

Christ's sacrificial death on the cross is the only basis acceptable to God for the forgiveness of our sins. Jesus could be that sacrifice because He is God in the flesh. From His own mouth come the words, "Sacrifice and offering You did not desire, but a body You have prepared for Me" (Hebrews 10:5). And in the same letter to the Hebrews that declaration is followed by the words, "By that will we have been sanctified through the offering of the body of Jesus Christ once for all" (Hebrews 10:10).

2) Jesus Christ bore all our sins on the cross.

Jesus Christ, who knew no sin, became sin for us (II Corinthians 5:21). He took our sins upon Himself. On the cross the Father in heaven "laid on Him the iniquity of us all" (Isaiah 53:6). "He Himself bore our sins in His own body on the tree" (I Peter 2:24), and thus He is the very foundation for the forgiveness of sins.

3) Jesus Christ alone gains our forgiveness.

The third facet of the content of faith for forgiveness is that the death of the Son of God on the cross counts with God for us all. It was *His* death alone, no one else's, that could result in forgiveness for all. All others have themselves been subject to death and under its authority. Jesus alone was above the authority of death. His virgin birth is of utmost consequence here, for because of this, even in His humanity He was not subject to death's authority—and He alone was born of a virgin. Jesus did die, but He submitted to death of His own free will.

Abraham, Sarah, David, Elisha, Daniel, Zachariah, Elizabeth, and John the Baptist were among the finest people who have ever lived. But great as they were, their deaths could not qualify as a sacrifice for sin—not even for themselves. The deaths of these people, or the death of anyone other than Christ, could do nothing to atone for the sin and guilt of humanity. That is a task only God could accomplish.

It takes God to die as a sacrifice for human sins, but divine nature itself cannot die. Therefore, it was necessary that God become man in order to die. As one great theologian of the early Church said, "We needed an incarnate God; God put to death, that we might live." In the mystery of the incarnation, the Son of God became a man, assuming human nature, so He could die for the sins of the whole world. Jesus was born to die.

Faith leading to forgiveness has content, and that content includes the death of the incarnate God in His flesh, bearing our sins as our sacrifice for sin, as well as faith in His resurrection and His dwelling in us by the power of the Holy Spirit. And that faith needs to translate into faithfulness on our part in our lives and the bearing of the fruits of faith—without which our faith weakens and even perhaps dies.

Obedience

Obedience is the fourth concrete action necessary for forgiveness. Obedience itself is part of the dynamic process of progress in the Christian's life. Faith dies when obedience fails. When faith fails, the fruit of forgiveness is forfeited.

Technically, we might say obedience isn't required for forgiveness, rather it is the fruit of forgiveness. Fair enough. But the fact is, when obedience to God is not forthcoming, the faith to believe for forgiveness drifts away like a boat loosed from its mooring.

Obedience has two elements: 1) the *desire* to obey, and 2) the positive *effort* to actually pursue the will of God. Our obedience may never become perfect, but the *desire* to make it perfect must be in place, as well as *effort* to act accordingly.

But remember, perfection isn't static. It has stages—like a baby's life. A three-month-old baby may not be perfect in maturity like a thirty-year-old man. But a three-month-old baby can be perfect for a three-month-old. Likewise, our obedience can be perfect for our current stage of spiritual development.

Know also that obedience is not blind submissiveness. It is, quite to the contrary, an active participation on our part with the energies of God. In love for God and in faith we *do* the things of God. Thus obedience is broad and not limited to one unbendable thing we must seek out and do.

Those four actions—repentance, confession, faith, and obedience—are indispensable for forgiveness of sins. Christ had done all for us in His birth, death, resurrection, and ascension, but we, with the help of God, engage ourselves to cooperate with Him, as the Scriptures teach, to carry out His will.

How to Receive God's Grace for Forgiveness

God gives grace freely. But His grace doesn't just float down to us through the air. He bestows it through channels, or vehicles, as it were—things like the Tree of Life in Eden, an ark, a serpent on a pole, a river, bread, and wine. The number of those vehicles is perhaps limitless. The Church calls those vehicles of the grace of God *sacraments*, or more accurately, mysteries. More will be said in the next chapter about the sacraments of the Church. Here it is sufficient to emphasize that the full and abiding fruit of forgiveness is not experienced apart from the sacraments, particularly those of baptism and the Eucharist (Holy Communion). In these mysteries grace for forgiveness is communicated to us.

The Bible is clear about the relationship between baptism and forgiveness. On the Day of Pentecost the people called out to the Apostles concerning their salvation, "Men and brethren, what shall we do?" And Peter said to them, "Repent, and let every one of you be baptized in the name of Jesus Christ *for the remission of sins*; and you shall receive the gift of the Holy Spirit" (Acts 2:37, 38, italics mine). Baptism and forgiveness of sins were linked for good on Day One of the Church. They cannot and must not be separated from each other. Baptism is foundational for forgiveness. In it you were brought into a new agreement, a new covenant with God, in which the forgiveness of your sins is part of God's promise to you.

In Holy Communion, too, there is grace for forgiveness. On the night of the Last Supper Jesus said of the cup, "Drink from it, all of you. For this is My blood of the new covenant, which is shed for many *for the remission of sins*" (Matthew 26:27, 28, italics mine). In Communion we partake of the Lamb of God who takes away the sin of the world. In the Orthodox Church, the bread of the Eucharist is even called "the Lamb"!

Some of the most sincere Christians I know, people who earnestly desire to overcome sin, have virtually no access to Communion. Or perhaps it's a quarterly affair. That won't do. We need that Communion regularly. It's part of the grace of forgiveness.

I'll flatly state that few people, if any, will ever overcome sin without the grace of forgiveness which is in baptism and Holy Communion. We're not talking about formality here. We're talking about life and victory through God's provision. Baptism and the Eucharist are not the inventions of men. They are the gifts of God Himself, taught by our Lord Jesus Christ, testified to in the Scriptures, and known through the centuries in the experience of the Church.

The Meaning of Forgiveness

The meaning of forgiveness is broad and deep, and its full

scope unfathomable. But there are some specifics we can understand about its meaning.

The very root meaning of the Greek verb for forgive is "to let go." God, when we repent, confess, and believe, lets our sins go! He does not hold them against us. He says, "Their sins and their lawless deeds I will remember no more" (Hebrews 10:17). (This is what God calls upon us to do when we forgive others of their transgressions against us: let them go and remember them no more!)

A closer look at the extent of what God has done and will do about our sins makes a beautiful picture. Consider three facts: 1) God *cleanses* us from our sins, 2) He *pardons* our sins, and 3) He *heals* the consequences of our sins.

Let me illustrate. Many years ago our family lived in Atlanta, Georgia. I was involved in a collegiate ministry which resulted in many of the players on the Georgia Tech football team becoming close, personal friends. My kids, the oldest of whom was thirteen at the time, reaped some benefits from this and had the unusual opportunity to play football with the "big boys" when they came over to our home.

So let's say the big kids are going down to the nearest playground to play a game of touch football. The field is wet and muddy. I say to my oldest, "Daniel, don't you go down there with those big guys. It's too dangerous. You'll get hurt." But he disobeys me and goes. He gets squished between two of the 250-plus pounders and ends up flat on the ground with a compound fracture of one of his legs.

The guys come and get me, and we go to the playground. There is my boy, broken bones protruding—blood and mud everywhere.

Now what would I do in such an event? Well, first off, I

wouldn't say, "You stupid brat. I told you not to play with those guys. It's your own fault. You can just lie there and suffer. It's time you learn to obey."

Even though he disobeyed, I'd do everything I could to help him. I'd rush him to the hospital in the safest way possible. Once there, at least three things would need to happen to take care of the problem in its complexity. First, the wound must be cleansed. Second, though not necessarily in that order, there must be pardon for his disobedience. That's between him and me. At some point he's going to have to say something to the effect, "Daddy, I'm sorry I disobeyed you." And I'm going to have to reply, "Sonny boy, I forgive you."

But cleansing the wound and pardoning the disobedience aren't all that's needed in such a situation. Going through life with a sterile compound fracture and a good relationship with your father isn't all that wonderful. A third thing must happen. The bones need setting and the wound has to be patched up. Healing is needed.

So it is with our sins. We need cleansing. Sin sullies; it dirties, and that moral dirt needs spiritual scrubbing, as it were. Without cleansing, moral and spiritual infection set in quickly. We need pardon for our sins. The guilt needs to be dealt with in order to prevent estrangement from God. But cleansing and pardoning aren't enough. There must also be a healing. Sin produces not only dirt and guilt, but also brokenness, sickness, and weakness. There needs to be a healing of the heart, the attitudes, even the personality. Without all three we will never know victory over our sinful passions.

All three of these—cleansing, pardoning, and healing— God has provided in His incarnate Son, Jesus Christ. There is cleansing through the blood of Christ. There is pardon in

Christ's sacrificial death. There is healing in our communion with Christ in the Holy Spirit. With this in view, it is plain to see why the following prayer to the Holy Trinity is one of the most often prayed prayers in the Orthodox Church:

> O Most Holy Trinity, have mercy on us. O Lord, cleanse us from our sins. O Master, pardon our iniquities. O Holy One, visit and heal our infirmities, for Your Name's sake.

God's forgiveness, His remitting of our sins, is not limited to this life only. All His forgiveness—with its cleansing, pardoning, and healing—have as their goal life everlasting. The knowledge of that is of great help in the battle here and now.

Chapter Seven

DIVINE ENERGY FOR HUMAN LIVING

For if we have been united together in the likeness of His death, certainly we also shall be in the likeness of His resurrection, knowing this, that our old man was crucified with Him, that the body of sin might be done away with, that we should no longer be slaves of sin. For he that has died has been freed from sin. —Romans 6:5-7

As marvelous and important as forgiveness is in our unseen warfare against sin, it does not by itself provide the totality of strength to overcome besetting sins. That's not the function of forgiveness. God has provided something else for that: union with His beloved Son. Our union with Christ is the very heart of our salvation. And all effective living as a Christian proceeds from being joined to Jesus Christ.

The purpose of this chapter is to consider the meaning of union with Christ and what that union has to do with being a vital Christian. Three questions must be answered to bring the issue clearly into perspective. First, what does it mean to be in union with Christ? Second, how do we come into that union? Third, how are we sustained in that union?

The Meaning of Union with Christ

Being united to Christ means that we, in our human nature, are joined into union with Christ in His human nature. We are grafted into Christ in His humanity (Romans 11:23). Jesus illustrated this clearly when He described Himself as the true vine and Christians as branches: "I am the true vine, and My Father is the vinedresser. Every branch in Me that does not bear fruit He takes away; and every branch that bears fruit He prunes, that it may bear more fruit. . . . Abide in Me, and I in you. As the branch cannot bear fruit of itself, unless it abides in the vine, neither can you, unless you abide in Me. I am the vine, you are the branches. He who abides in Me, and I in him, bears much fruit; for without Me you can do nothing" (John 15:1, 2, 4, 5).

The branches of a vine, of course, have exactly the same nature as the vine itself. There is an organic union between branches and vine. They are made out of the same stuff, and are joined together.

Picture a grapevine in your mind. Now, mentally put your finger on a place where the vine stops and a branch starts. It can't always be done, can it? The branches of a vine are part of the vine. The individual parts—branches, stalk, leaves—are together all part of the vine. Every branch participates in the vine's nature, getting its life from the vine.

So it is with Christians, the branches, and Jesus Christ, the vine. In union with Him, we share the exact same human nature He has, and we draw our life from Him. That is because His humanity is life-giving—life-giving because it is joined to

God the Son.

It is important to know that we are not joined with Christ in His divine nature. Were that the case that would make us, as it were, members of the Trinity. That's impossible!

Furthermore, in union with Christ, our human person is not mingled with His divine person. As we have said before, were that to occur, both He and we would lose our personal identity, and become some expression of person not previously in existence. Personness can't mingle, either in God or in man. A married man and woman, for instance, never become one person, but rather one flesh (Matthew 19:5). Person is always irreducible and distinctive. It can't be altered.

Then if we aren't joined to Christ in His divine nature and we aren't joined to Christ in His person, how are we joined to Him?

We are joined to Christ in His human nature, humanity that has been energized, divinized, by His divine nature. To come to God we need a mediator, a go-between, who relates to both God and man. Only the Lord Jesus Christ, God incarnate, true God and true man, qualifies to be that mediator. He relates to God in His deity and to mankind in His humanity. This is in part why the Apostle Paul could write to Timothy, "For there is one God and one Mediator between God and men, the Man Christ Jesus" (I Timothy 2:5).

There are at least five aspects of our union with Christ.

1) The union is real

Union with Christ is no ethereal, super secret, abstract religious idea. And it is not legal fiction, something God juridically declares to be true even though in fact there is no substance underlying that declaration. The Christian is truly, substantially in union with Jesus Christ in His humanity. This means that the stuff or substance of our human nature is joined with the substance of His human nature, and the two become one, ours being joined to His. In Bible terms, we are bone of His bone, and flesh of His flesh (Genesis 2:23).

How this union occurs is a mystery; *that* it happens is a reality. We can live and participate in it now, though only in eternity, in the fullness of the kingdom of God, may we discover all it means for us to be in union with Christ. But that this union is substantial or real we can know about here and now.

2) His death is our death

In union with Christ, His death becomes the death of all joined to Him. That should not be difficult to grasp. If I am joined to one who dies, it should be quite evident I necessarily die with that one. If I don't, there was not a true union. Thinking back to the vine and branch illustration, that would be like saying the vine died but the branches lived on. It is not possible for a vine to die while its branches keep on living. If a vine dies, all the branches joined to it die, too.

So it is with the person who has been grafted into union with Christ. In Christ, "you died, and your life is hidden with Christ in God" (Colossians 3:3). Therefore, death has no more power over us (Romans 6:9), for in being joined to Christ, we already participate in His death. We have and are putting off the old man; we are putting on the new.

It is precisely because Paul was united to Christ he could say, "I have been crucified with Christ" (Galatians 2:20). Or again, regarding baptism, "For if we have been united together in the likeness of His death, certainly we also shall be in the likeness of His resurrection, knowing this, that our old man was crucified with Him" (Romans 6:5, 6).

3) His resurrection is our new birth

Being united to Christ in His death is but the beginning of the benefits of union with Him. There is so much more. Jesus Christ did not remain in the grave. He rose from the dead. Obviously, then, those united to Him are also raised with Him. What other reasonable conclusion could we draw? If a vine dies, all its branches die. If that vine miraculously comes back to life, its branches come back to life. Thus Paul not only said, "I have been crucified with Christ," but also, "nevertheless I live."

Once again, be sure you understand that our death and resurrection in Christ are not symbolic, nor do we refer to some hypothetical or figurative way God views us. In Christ we have died and have been raised from the dead as surely as Christ has died and has been raised from the dead. This is reality. Saint Paul simply assumes the Colossians have been raised with Christ when he writes, "If then you were raised with Christ, seek those things which are above, where Christ is sitting at the right hand of God" (Colossians 3:1). We have begun to participate in His death and resurrection—all this aiming at the ultimate participation, our resurrection at the second and glorious coming and life with Him forever and ever.

4) He is our energy source

The consequences of union with Christ go even beyond death and resurrection with Him. Access to His glorified humanity is included. Specifically here I mean those divine energies.

Just as the strength of a branch is not in itself apart from the vine, so our strength is not in ourselves but in our Vine. A branch cut off from the vine has no life, and it has no strength. But remaining united to the vine it receives the energy of the vine flowing through it. Remember the sword in the fire? The heat or energy of the fire interpenetrate the steel sword to make it red hot. So it is in our union with Christ. Empowered by the divinized humanity of Jesus Christ to which we are joined, we can enter the battle—and win.

So much strength is available to us in union with Christ that Paul could boldly claim, "I can do all things through Christ who strengthens me" (Philippians 4:13). And Jesus said, "Without Me you can do nothing" (John 14:6), the apparent implication being that united to Him we can do everything He calls us to do. Both statements make it evident that in union with Christ we are enabled to operate with a new strength, strength which becomes ours through Him. Union with Christ is the bottom line for Christian living.

5) We are in process toward total renewal

Union with Christ should affect the totality of the lives of those joined to Him. However, we won't realize the full extent of its fruits immediately. There is a process to be experienced here. The whole you is *being* renewed (Colossians 3:10).

We experience renewal inwardly one way, and outwardly, or physically, another. There is a growth process in progress in us as a result of our union with Christ.

When a baby is born it possesses the nature of its parents. Human parents have human babies. The baby is fully alive and fully human, but it's not fully developed. The infant will never be any more or any less human, and it will never have any more or any less human nature. The potential is all there, but it's going to take a lot of food, sleep, exercise, time—and whatever else—before it is going to be fully mature and its potential realized. So it is with the Christian in union with Christ.

Inward renewal should be a continual process throughout all our lives. But such is not the case with our physical bodies, though they too will one day realize the full effect of that union with Christ. Saint Paul encouraging the Corinthians wrote in this regard: "Therefore we do not lose heart. Even though our outward man is perishing, yet the inward man is being renewed day by day" (II Corinthians 4:16). And to the Romans he wrote, "And if Christ is in you, the body is dead because of sin, but the Spirit is life because of righteousness. But if the Spirit of Him who raised Jesus from the dead dwells in you, He who raised Christ from the dead will also give life to your mortal bodies through His Spirit who dwells in you" (Romans 8:10, 11).

For those in union with Christ, transformation inwardly is a process. But the mortal body won't be changed until a future time when Christ returns to this earth for those who are His. We read, "Behold, I tell you a mystery: We shall not all sleep, but we shall all be changed—in a moment, in the twinkling of an eye, at the last trumpet. For the trumpet will sound, and the dead will be raised incorruptible, and we shall be changed" (I Corinthians 15:51, 52).

How Union with Christ is Established

When was the last time you heard someone talk about being born again? For many, the expression "born again" is a catch-all for any experience one sees as beginning a relationship with God. The expression "born again," accurately used, however, refers to coming into union with Christ.

How, then, do we come into union with Christ? That is, how are we born again?

Let's start with two ways it doesn't happen. First, no one just happens inadvertently to come into union with Christ. It is no accident. You don't wake up one morning and discover that you were born again during the night. Rather, it is quite a deliberate occurrence.

Second, no one puts himself or herself into union with Christ. You can't "born yourself again." We are "... born, not of blood, nor of the will of the flesh, nor of the will of man, but of God" (John 1:13). You cannot regenerate yourself in Christ any more than you can "born yourself" as a baby.

So what is the occasion of someone's coming into union with Christ? Where and how does the new birth occur?

Suppose a young man and young woman meet. The relationship progresses to the point at which the two of them believe they are sincerely and deeply in love with each other, and they are convinced beyond doubt they are committed to each other. They decide on this basis to live together. They have three beautiful children, and spend the rest of their lives together—as unlikely as that usually proves to be! But they skip one bit of business—they don't bother to get married.

Do they experience any of the aspects of marriage?

Of course they do.

Is there any genuine union between them?

The Bible's answer to that is affirmative. (See I Corinthians 6:15, 16.)

Could such a relationship in time be considered a legal

marriage?

Surely. There is such a thing as a common-law marriage. But are they really and truly married? No! Cohabitation is not marriage. And common-law marriage is a legal accommodation, not true marriage. The arrangement is neither proper nor normal. The relationship lacks something as plain as day: a wedding!

Suppose some fifteen years down the line this couple realizes the impropriety and abnormality of their relationship. Should something be done at this late date about the lack of a wedding? Absolutely. And until they do, not only do they lack the blessing of God in the relationship, they lack the grace of God they need to live as married. That lack, as long as it exists, will be detrimental to them, to their children, and to the society in which they live.

Born again—when?

Just as there is a normal and proper occasion to establish a union between a man and a woman, marriage, so there is a normal and proper occasion to establish union with Jesus Christ. That occasion is *baptism.* Marriage establishes a union between a man and a woman. Baptism establishes a union between a man or a woman and Jesus Christ.

This biblical truth may come as a surprise to many sincere Christian people who are in a religious environment that views baptism as a kind of helpful thing, for whatever reason, but certainly not essential—other than as an act of obedience to Christ. They regard baptism as "an outward sign of an inward act." That is not what the Scriptures teach.

For a marriage, the sacramental ceremony is a whole lot more than a helpful but unnecessary outward sign of some solemn inner act. Similarly, baptism is infinitely more than a pleasant outward sign of a private inner transformation. It is God's prescribed means to union with Christ.

The Bible teaches, and the Church has practiced since the Day of Pentecost, baptism as God's normal and proper occasion for being joined to Christ. Look at what Saint Paul says in Romans 6:1-7:

> What shall we say then? Shall we continue in sin that grace may abound? Certainly not! How shall we who died to sin live any longer in it? Or do you not know that as many of us as were baptized into Christ Jesus were baptized into His death? Therefore we were buried with Him through baptism into death, that just as Christ was raised from the dead by the glory of the Father, even so we also should walk in newness of life. For if we have been united together in the likeness of His death, certainly we also shall be in the likeness of His resurrection, knowing this, that our old man was crucified with Him, that the body of sin might be done away with, that we should no longer be slaves of sin. For he who has died has been freed from sin.

The birth from above and baptism were forever inseparably linked together by Jesus when He said, "Most assuredly, I say to you, unless one is born of water and the Spirit, he cannot enter the kingdom of God" (John 3:5). One must ignore the obvious meaning of words to make water here refer to anything but baptism.

Interestingly, almost all Christians who don't agree that baptism is God's normal way to the new birth do agree that some "event" must occur for the new birth to happen. Ask people who profess to be born again how that occurred and some will reply, "I invited Jesus to come into my life." With others it's, "I went forward at a meeting." Still others name a time when, in prayer to God, they confessed their sins and asked Him to save them. These are a few of the ways people today believe they are born again.

None of these events are bad in themselves. But they aren't mentioned in the Bible. Baptism is—over and over again—precisely in the context of people initially coming into a relationship with God. Perhaps a Protestant reaction to certain Roman Catholic abuses is at the root of substitution of other events for baptism. This reaction is understandable in the light of history. But proper practice must be based on revelation, not reaction; it must be founded solidly on truth.

Furthermore, anyone who approaches union with Christ by some occasion other than baptism, even in the utmost sincerity and faith, and has never been baptized, needs to be baptized once he becomes aware that baptism is God's way. There is grace from God he will lack without baptism.

I think it needs to be mentioned here that most of those who believe baptism is not important to being born again are totally insistent on a marriage ceremony before living together. Perhaps this inconsistency is one of the reasons why so many young people see no need for a marriage before living to-gether. If the rite of holy baptism is merely symbolic, why not the rite of holy matrimony? Christians, take note. Is it we who have helped to make the certificate "just a piece of paper"?

Baptism: normal—other means: abnormal
Should you still wonder whether baptism is God's normal

and proper occasion for our being placed into union with Christ, consider again the Day of Pentecost. Peter said to those asking how they could be saved, "Repent, and let every one of you be baptized in the name of Jesus Christ for the remission of sins; and you shall receive the gift of the Holy Spirit" (Acts 2:38). Baptism was *the* event for union with Christ for those who responded to Christ through Peter's preaching that day. I assure you, there was no one in the crowd at Pentecost saying within himself, "Hmmm, I like this message, but this baptism thing sure isn't necessary. I'll just raise my hand and ask Jesus into my heart. That will do the job for me." Incredible! But it's done all the time these days.

At Pentecost there wasn't a hint of people inviting Jesus into their hearts and lives, going forward, or checking a card. Years later, Peter wrote, "baptism now saves you—not the removal of dirt from the flesh, but an appeal to God for a good conscience—through the resurrection of Jesus Christ" (I Peter 3:21; NASB).

The question of baptism, of course, has provoked widespread debate—particularly since the Protestant Reformation. All sides in the discussion claim their viewpoint is derived from Scripture. However, many Christians are not aware that the preponderance of the historic Church's understanding of the biblical teaching about baptism from the very beginning, and through all of her centuries, is that baptism is God's chosen vehicle whereby the Holy Spirit brings us into union with Jesus Christ, that is, by which we are born again.

This is not to say that baptism "automatically" insures heaven. Baptism no more guarantees a successful Christian experience than a marriage ceremony guarantees a successful marriage. But without baptism, there is an abnormality in our relationship with God. As the marriage ceremony is the beginning of a successful, healthy marriage, so baptism is the starting point of a normal and proper relationship with Jesus Christ. Is there any doubt that this is what the Apostles practiced as recorded for us in the Scriptures?

Union with Christ Needs Nurture

Baptism, then, is the beginning of union with Christ. But the new birth needs nurture. A newborn infant does not stand six feet tall and weigh 180 pounds. A child doesn't run a four-minute mile at four years—or fourteen years. People are born tiny and need nurture to grow and gain strength and endurance. Even as there is a need for time and nurture in human growth after physical birth, nurture and time is needed in order to advance in spiritual maturity after spiritual birth. Strength, endurance, and maturity develop in our union with Christ with proper time and consistent nurture.

In His love for us, God has provided means of grace to nurture that union. The reading and contemplation of the Holy Scriptures is one of the finest. Listening to sound biblical preaching and fellowship with others who are in union with Christ are both greatly beneficial. Add to that the singing of hymns and prayer, and you've got still more means by which Christians are nurtured. These vehicles—but a few of many—provide for our growth in union with Christ.

Really what we are talking about here is the sacramental life of the Church, the physical side of being spiritual. There are many concrete, physical actions by which God's people experience spiritual life. Baptism, for instance, is a sacrament. Marriage is a sacrament. Anointing with oil is a sacrament. Other sacraments include healing, ordination,

Holy Communion—physical ways in which God imparts magnificent grace to His people. The Lord knows, we need them all!

The best means of nurture

Of the means for spiritual nurture, God has provided one which I have mentioned is higher than all the others—one that is absolutely, totally, and completely indispensable if union with Christ is to be lived out in its fullness. Call it the Lord's Table, Holy Communion, the Lord's Supper, the Eucharist (which means *thanksgiving*), it is the partaking of the body and blood of the Lord Jesus Christ. This is *the* means which God has given for consistent nurture in the Christian life. The Eucharist has been called the Sacrament of sacraments; the Mystery of the mysteries. It is *the* event for nurture.

Just as there is no substitute in a Christian life for the Scriptures, prayer, and fellowship, so also there is no substitute for the Eucharist. (I choose to use the term Eucharist because thanksgiving to God for what He has done, and is doing in imparting to us His very own Son, is the best description of what is going on in this event.)

The Scriptures plainly tell us why the Eucharist is so utterly crucial to spiritual growth for a person in union with the incarnate Christ. The Lord Himself said, "Take, eat, this is My body . . . this is my blood . . ." (Matthew 26:26, 28). At His Supper we partake of Him in His glorified humanity. His body and blood are gifts to us for nurture, strength, and growth as Christians.

But let's ask the tough questions. How can it be that bread and wine are His body and blood? To be dogmatically honest, I don't know! It is the work of the Holy Spirit, and it defies explanation. We know *that* it is His body and blood, for He said so. *How* it is, we cannot tell. The Fathers of the ancient Church employed an expression to explain how the bread and wine became the body and blood of Christ. It translates into three words in our language: "O great mystery!" And a mystery it is indeed.

Do the bread and wine of the Eucharist chemically become Jesus' flesh and blood? Some claim it is so, but that's a speculative attempt to explain the mystery. It remains a mystery. And how we are nurtured is a mystery, but nurture us in Christ it does.

Many sincerely ask, "Aren't the bread and wine only symbols?" Yes, they are symbols. But not symbols *only*. And they are not symbols that stand for something they aren't. Let me explain. These symbols participate in Christ's glorified body and blood, and those who partake in faith of these gifts really do partake of the body and blood of Christ. They are His body and blood. Jesus taught, "Most assuredly, I say to you, unless you eat the flesh of the Son of Man and drink His blood, you have no life in you" (John 6:53). John reports that the result of this teaching of the Lord was that "from that time many of His disciples went back and walked with Him no more" (John 6:66).

The disciples who left Jesus that day weren't the Twelve. Those who left were part of a wider circle of disciples who had followed Him up to that point in His ministry. But they were deeply offended when He said, "For My flesh is food indeed, and My blood is drink indeed. He who eats My flesh and drinks My blood abides in Me, and I in him" (John 6:55, 56). They were not offended by some empty symbolic idea. They were affronted because they knew He meant the real thing, and they understood

110

what He meant, but simply could not handle it and left Him. There are some who do this today as well.

If there is any question whether or not the bread and wine of the Eucharist, the Communion, is the body and blood of the Lord, the Last Supper discourse of Jesus should forever settle the matter. We commonly read it in Paul's words in I Corinthians 11:23-27.

> For I received from the Lord that which I also delivered to you: that the Lord Jesus on the same night in which He was betrayed took bread; and when He had given thanks, He broke it and said, "Take, eat; this is My body which is broken for you; do this in remembrance of Me." In the same manner He also took the cup after supper, saying, "This cup is the new covenant in My blood. This do, as often as you drink it, in remembrance of Me." For as often as you eat this bread and drink this cup, you proclaim the Lord's death till He comes. Therefore whoever eats this bread or drinks this cup of the Lord in an unworthy manner will be guilty of the body and blood of the Lord.

The primary means of nurture for those who have been born again is the Eucharist. There we partake of the living Son of God in His glorified human nature. It is a holy meal at the holy table of the holy God—a meal which we partake of in the heavenlies, the Kingdom of God, the Age to come, even while living in this age. The sustenance gained at that meal in dining with Him and partaking of Him is of infinitely greater importance to our lives in union with Christ than are our daily meals to our physical bodies.

BACK TO THE BASICS

Summary

Union with Jesus Christ is the energy source for Christian living because being joined to Him we participate in His glorified humanity. We have access to a transformed humanity. God has provided a way for us to enter into that union, baptism, and He has provided nurture for growth in the life of that union through the sacramental life of the Church, particularly in Holy Communion. It is in this union that strength is gained to engage successfully in spiritual battle.

Chapter Eight

THE SWORD IN THE FIRE

...By which have been given to us exceedingly great and precious promises, that through these you may be partakers of the divine nature, having escaped the corruption that is in the world through lust. —II Peter 1:4

The birth from above unites us to Christ and equips us for "all things that pertain to life and godliness, through the knowledge of Him who called us by glory and virtue" (II Peter 1:3). Being joined to Christ in His glorified humanity makes available a new power source to us. In this chapter we'll consider that potential of power accessible to us through union with Christ. We will turn our attention again to the two natures in Christ, that is, His divine nature and His human nature. Two critical questions will be considered: 1) How do those two natures relate in Him? and 2) What does that relationship have to do with us?

Another Look at Christ's Two Natures
Let us start with the relationship between the divine and

human natures of Christ.

First, those two natures do not mingle so as to become one nature, for this would make Him part God and part man. Don't forget that ever-so-crucial line from the Council of Chalcedon: ". . . in two natures, without confusion [mixing], without change, without division, without separation . . ."

Second, it is also important we do not understand the union of those two natures in Christ as existing closely but independently of each other—as, for example, the gluing of two blocks of wood together side by side. This would inevitably lead to the false conclusion that His two natures don't really work together, but that He always must use one or the other. The incarnate Son works in both natures. Christ's divine nature wasn't put on "hold" while He walked here on earth, and the human nature isn't on "hold" now that He is in heaven at the right hand of the Father.

Third, though the two natures never co-mingle, there is a powerful effect of His divine nature upon His human nature. It is on that effect we need to focus now.

The sword in the fire reconsidered

Remember the sword in the fire illustration in chapter five? The aim there was simply to show that the human and divine natures in Christ do not mingle but rather stay distinct, though not separate. Now we'll go a step further and apply the sword in the fire as an illustration of what strength is available to us when we are joined to Christ.

To expand upon this ancient example, you heat a sword in a fire until it's white hot. Then you dip it in a tub of water. What happens? The hot sword makes the water sputter and hiss. Or, if the red-hot sword is pressed against a piece of wood, the wood will scorch—perhaps even burst into flames.

Let us make two observations from this illustration. First, fire has one kind of nature and iron a nature quite distinct from it. It is the nature of a sharpened sword to cut; it is the nature of fire to burn. Yet, now the heated sword can both cut and burn. The heat of the fire penetrates the sword. The sword does not become fire by nature. But it does participate in the heat, the energy, of the fire. Through all this, though, both the fire and the sword maintain their distinct natures.

Now, is it the fire or the sword that burns the wood which the sword touches? The answer is *both*. Once the sword participates in the heat of the fire, it can inflict a burn quite easily. The energy produced by the fire is passed on to the sword and heat becomes a characteristic of the sword as well as of the fire. It is accurate to say that the fire burns *through* the sword. And it is every bit as correct to say that the sword itself burns the wood with heat from the fire.

Now apply the illustration to Christ. The fire represents His divine nature, the sword His human nature. Just as fire affects steel with its energy, so, through the union of those two natures in the one person of the Son of God, the divine nature affects His human nature with its divine energies. His human nature participates in the uncreated energies, or qualities, of the divine nature. As a result, the Lord Jesus Christ in His humanity lived and acted as a man exercising divine qualities in His humanity. As a man He was a powerful, living demonstration—an icon—of the manner in which God, from the very beginning, intended all people to live.

Divine energies

As light and heat radiate from fire but are not fire by

nature, yet are energies of fire, so there are energies that radiate, as it were, from divine nature, but are not the essence of the divine nature itself. People joined to Christ have access to those energies because of their union with Him in His now glorified humanity. That union produces a transformation in our nature. Saint Paul wrote of this when he said, "If anyone is in Christ, he is a new creation; old things have passed away; behold, all things have become new" (II Corinthians 5:17). To be "in Christ" is to be united to Christ. Part of our transformation is the privilege of partaking in the divine energies.

So how does all this happen? How does humanity come to participate in deity?

There was and is in Jesus Christ a never-ceasing *interpenetration* of His human nature by the divine nature. It could not be any other way. As a sword enveloped in fire cannot avoid being heated because it is of the nature of fire to heat, so humanity cannot be "enveloped" by deity without being energized by deity. So without *mixing,* without *change,* without *division,* and without *separation,* there was *interpenetration.* Christ's humanity was energized by His divinity. Humanity was made to participate in deity.

This was not a matter of the divine nature merely "expressing itself" through passive human nature. Rather, this was the Son of God, His human nature interpenetrated by His divine nature, actively expressing Himself in both natures. Jesus did not just "appear to" or "seem to" operate as a man. That is heresy. He operated in actuality as a man, through "divinized" humanity.

Becoming partakers of the divine nature

This "divinization" of the human nature by the divine

116

doesn't stop with Christ, however. It begins with Him, but in Christ the foundation is laid for a corresponding impact on our lives. In His humanity Christ became the first-born among many brethren—the beginning of a new human family, a family with a whole new set of capabilities. We enter into that family through the new birth. We are united with Christ in His human nature and thus, obviously, we are united to One whose humanity is interpenetrated by the divine nature. This union with Him provides access to the same divine qualities He has in His humanity.

What a new world of possibilities for us as Christians in our war against sin! In union with Christ, we can, amongst many things, wage a winning war against temptation, against passions, and against demonic foes. We can become, as Paul promises, "more than conquerors" (Romans 8:37). This is why Peter could write, "His divine power has given to us all things that pertain to life and godliness, through the knowledge of Him who called us by glory and virtue, by which have been given to us exceedingly great and precious promises, that through these you may be partakers of the divine nature, having escaped the corruption that is in the world through lust" (II Peter 1:3, 4).

Don't think Peter's thought here was that being "partakers of the divine nature" means we become one nature directly with the divine nature, co-mingled with the nature of the almighty, eternal, and everlasting God. Instead, it is that we, in our redeemed humanity, because we are joined to Christ, participate in the qualities, or energies, of God.

Jesus made possible for us the end of our frustration, that is of being unable to be what we are intended to be in the purpose of God. This He did by incorporating us into Himself,

117

thereby making God's energies available to our human nature.

Because you are made in God's image, you are capable of containing and exercising God's uncreated energies. Uncreated love, joy, and peace are such qualities. You can't "manufacture" these on your own, they are gifts from God. They come by participation in God.

You noticed the adjective *uncreated* for those energies. We're not talking here of a love, joy, or peace that God has created and which all people can exercise. This is love, joy, and peace that is natural to God Himself and thus uncreated. This is God's love, joy, and peace that radiate, as it were, from the nature of God, and in which through Christ we can participate.

The role of the Holy Spirit in our union with Christ

In chapter seven we said God's normal and proper "event" for us to come into union with Christ is baptism, and that this union is primarily nurtured in Holy Communion. It's not the water by itself in baptism that accomplishes this union. It is the Holy Spirit *in* the water. And it is not alone the bread and wine of the Eucharist that impart grace. It is the action of the Holy Spirit in the bread and wine. The Holy Spirit effects our union with Christ, and the Holy Spirit maintains it.

It is also the Holy Spirit who is active in this "energizing" of the Christian through union with Christ. Actually, all three persons of the Trinity are active because they always act together. As you will recall, we have already taken note of a classical formula for this personal action of the Holy Trinity: *from* the Father, *through* the Son, *in* the Spirit. Here we are focusing on "*in* the Spirit."

The Baptism in the Holy Spirit

We're all tired of the confusion and quibbling about the work of the Holy Spirit these days. Personally, I believe it is ignorance of the Church's rich historic teaching on this subject which is responsible for a great degree of abnormality in contemporary Christian teaching and experience. I think ignorance is also the cause of most of the current controversy about the nature of the work of the Holy Spirit, or the baptism of the Holy Spirit, or the filling of the Holy Spirit—people can't even agree on what to call it!

Both the modern charismatic movement, and the Pentecostal movement which preceded and overlapped it, have contributed significantly to the confusion. I'm not denying that there has been a need for more attention to the work of the Spirit in much of Christendom, and that the charismatic renewal may have been a source of spiritual encouragement to many. But the movement is flawed with many serious defects doctrinally and is certainly anything but united.

One issue in the current controversy about the Holy Spirit is the meaning of the expression *baptism in the Holy Spirit.* This is unfortunate and there needs to be some sober clarity here. This is no place for word games, or for saying what people believe is not important.

Historically, the receiving of the Holy Spirit has been connected with the sacrament of baptism, exactly as it was on the Day of Pentecost. The Apostle Peter, you recall, on that day told the people, "Repent and be baptized . . . and you will receive the gift of the Holy Spirit." Baptism into Christ and the baptism of the Holy Spirit went together. That day 5000 people were baptized in water and also baptized in the Holy Spirit at the hands of the Apostles.

For twenty centuries the Orthodox Church has continued this precise practice of linking together baptism and the gift of the Holy Spirit. Baptism in the Church is immediately followed by chrismation, a sacramental anointing with oil, imparting the gift of the Holy Spirit. Thus being born again, coming into union with Christ, and being baptized in the Holy Spirit are all part of the same experience as they were at Pentecost. No one need wonder, "Have I really received the gift of the Holy Spirit?" It's accomplished in the sacrament. That's God's normal way. You can act in faith on it. You need not be looking for some "ultimate spiritual experience" with the Holy Spirit. You go back to God's action through baptism and chrismation. There is no greater or "more ultimate" experience with God than being joined to Christ and receiving the gift of the Holy Spirit at baptism.

The baptism of the Holy Spirit is dynamic

Some say the baptism of the Holy Spirit is a second work of grace. That's bad theology. The gift of the Spirit must not be something second; it must be something *constant*. We know that if the Holy Spirit's work is to be real to us and in us at any given time in our lives as Christians, the gift of the Spirit must always be a present reality. And of course it is, for He is ever with us. His work is dynamic. That is, the Holy Spirit's baptism is on-going, continuous, day-by-day, minute-by-minute, never ceasing.

This is easy to understand if we go back to the sword and fire illustration once again. Steel doesn't retain the heat of a fire it was heated in five years ago. Nor can you walk in the energies of the divine nature on the basis of a spiritual experience at some past point in your life—as valid as it may have been—but which is not constantly being renewed. If we are to walk in the "white heat" of the qualities of the divine nature which are available to us, we must continually abide in Christ. That takes the gift of the Holy Spirit. No one-time experience of the Spirit's baptism is adequate to equip you to live and war each day against your spiritual foes. The idea of sporadic "booster shots" may be encouraging, but there cannot be enough of them to carry you through the nitty-gritty stuff of life.

In almost every service of the Orthodox Church a prayer is prayed to the Holy Spirit that expresses our need of the constant presence of the Holy Spirit in us. At the center of this prayer is the petition, "come abide in us . . ." This is a prayer for a constant, abiding Spirit. The experience of the Spirit's baptism must always be fresh.

Living as a Christian with New Capabilities

So far in this chapter we've considered the availability of the divine energies in our lives through union with Christ, and the work of the Holy Spirit in effecting that union with the consequent energizing of our nature. Now it's time to turn to specific practical implications of this incredible blessing of God in our everyday battle with sin.

Historically, the "battle plans" suggested for Christians have fallen under one of three basic models. First, there are two that don't work. The third does.

1) The "Boot-strappers"
Reach down and grab your shoes by the tongue. Now lift. Come on, harder! Are you walking on air yet? If not, you aren't pulling hard enough. If you strain a bit more, you may get yourself off the ground.

Sound foolish? Of course it does. But it's no more nonsensical than the idea that we, apart from God, are equipped with enough natural resources to fight a successful war against real spiritual enemies. Many, however, have insisted we are able, and their teaching I label "religious boot-strappers." It's the do-it-yourself approach to being a Christian. The bootstrappers are the self-help crowd gone pious, and they have incorrigible confidence in human nature. They are confident there is no foe they can't lick if they will put out enough discipline and effort. It's the old, "you can do what you want to do if you work hard enough at it" scheme. All you need to do is set your mind to it, and you'll make it.

It may sound challenging to be told you've inherently got it in you to defeat sin. Don't be deceived, you can't. It can't be done apart from those divine energies. Jesus demonstrated He thoroughly understood what human nature could or could not do when He said, "Apart from Me you can do nothing" (John 15:5). We must exercise those energies, and Christian living does require personal effort, but not apart from God's divine energies.

2) Channels only

Then there is a scheme for Christian living that is the exact opposite of boot-strap theology. I call it "channels-only theology." I mentioned this in chapter one as the "He'll do it all through you" key. Its adherents are totally pessimistic about human nature and view us all as worms crawling on the ground. Cruelly overstating the fall of man, they tell us that at best we'll never be able to be anything more than passive tubes through which God works. There's a hymn many of those committed to this program sing that captures their theology well. The chorus goes:

Channels only blessed Master,
But with all Thy wondrous power
Flowing through us Thou canst use us
Every day and every hour.

Channels-only theology was introduced to me when I was twenty-six and I heard a man say, "The Christian life is not a hard life to live; it's impossible. Only one person has ever lived the Christian life, and that was Jesus Christ. There is still only one person who can live the Christian life, and that is Jesus Christ. But now, if you step aside, He will live His life in you and through you. He will think through you, love through you, witness to Himself through you." I was already having a tough time living the Christian life, so if Christ would do it all for me, I was more than willing to let Him. Besides, it would be so much easier to have Him resist temptation for me, speak for me, and serve others for me, while I watched from the grandstands. That's vintage channels-only theology in practice.

Here's a quick glimpse into how channels-only theology is supposed to work, and part of it is correct. It agrees that God dwells in individual Christians, and that His grace does work actively through them. So far so good. But the problem is, this is as far as it goes. Christ must do *everything* in us from then on; we do nothing except believe. The consequences are passive, almost robotic Christians.

Say, for example, there are people you can't bear the sight of, but because you're a Christian you are desperately trying to love them. If channels-only theology is your persuasion you can say, "I don't love them—or even like them—but I'll trust Christ to love them through me." Or, "The Christ in me will love the Christ in them." Channels-only theology ignores the reality and stops short of the conclusion that "*I* need to love that person, and with God's help I will."

Channels-only theology is a tradition of men and is inadequate for Christian living because it fails to put footwork to faith. Failure for proper Christian conduct is blamed on lack of faith, never on the lack of obediently doing what ought to be done. You go through life berating yourself for lack of faith when that may not be the problem at all. It reduces Christian living to a matter of trying to believe God for something He never promised to do! Where in the New Testament did Jesus ever say he would live the Christian life for us? Jesus said, "Love your enemies" (Matthew 5:44), but He did not say He would love our enemies through us. It is our responsibility to believe in Him and then to love our enemies. He has equipped us to do that, and we must do what He has commanded.

Most adherents of channels-only theology are sincere Christians caught in the midst of contradictory doctrines. They are so skittish about the possibility of someone thinking he can earn salvation by his own works that they mentally throw out works altogether. In their earnest desire to follow Christ faithfully, they have fallen prey to a doctrinal passivity regarding responsible action on the part of the individual Christian. Their actions, incidentally, are seldom as passive as their doctrine.

In addition, they are usually so ardently anti-Roman Catholic that they have rejected what the Bible teaches on the sacraments, and cut themselves off from God's grace granted through them. *People* can be channels, but bread, wine, and water can't be? What a contradiction!

3) Working together with God

Okay, if we can't live as Christians in our own strength, and if Christ isn't going to live the Christian life for us, how do we go about living as Christians, especially in the light of the unseen warfare?

There is a way, and it does work. God does it, and we must do it too. We work together with God. We co-operate with God.

Back to the sword in the fire illustration once again. What causes wood to burn when touched by a heated sword? There are at least three correct answers: the fire, the heat, the sword.

It is inherent in the nature of fire to radiate heat, and thus it has the capacity to burn. It is not inherent in the nature of steel to radiate heat. But it is in the nature of steel to be able to participate in the heat of a fire and radiate that heat.

Similarly, energized by union with Christ, we have access to the qualities needed to be godly. Then we are capable of living God's way. A Christian energized, for example, with the love of God can love with divine love. It is possible to love our enemies, just as Christ commanded.

Living God's way is not just getting a bit of help from God, nor is it the old, "God is my co-pilot" scheme, where I'm in charge and He cooperates with me. It is me cooperating with Him. In cooperation there is *one* operation, but *two* parties working together. Our God and King works, and we, His servants, work with Him. In dynamic union with Christ, participating in the energies from God's own nature, we are able to work together with God. Look again at these words from II Peter 1:4-8:

... by which have been given to us exceedingly great and precious promises, that through these you may be partakers of the divine nature, having escaped the corruption that is in the world through lust. But also for this very reason, giving all diligence, add to your faith virtue, to virtue knowledge, to knowledge self-control, to self-control perseverance, to perseverance godliness, to godliness brotherly kindness, and to brotherly kindness love. For if these things are yours and abound, you will be neither barren nor unfruitful in the knowledge of our Lord Jesus Christ.

Where do those seven qualities—moral excellence, knowledge, self-control, perseverance, godliness, brotherly kindness, and love—come from? Are they the native equipment of all human beings? Yes and no. Yes, because being made in the image of God we have the capacity for them. No, because they don't operate in human nature without God any more than heat does in a steel sword unless heated by energy from outside of itself. We must produce them together with God. They become ours. "If these qualities are yours..." says Saint Peter.

A whole new world of capabilities opens up when we possess these divine qualities. Saint Paul writes, "I can do all things through Christ who strengthens me" (Philippians 4:13). Who does the doing? Paul does. In his own strength alone? Of course not. He does all things *through* Christ who strengthens him. That's not Christ doing all things through a passive Paul. Paul is doing all things, for Christ is strengthening him.

Look again at Galatians 2:20: "I have been crucified with Christ; it is no longer I who live, but Christ lives in me; and the life which I now live in the flesh I live by faith in the Son of

God, who loved me and gave Himself for me." Who is doing the living? Christ is; and Paul is too—because of his union with Christ.

Or consider, "Therefore, my beloved, as you have always obeyed, not as in my presence only, but now much more in my absence, work out your own salvation with fear and trembling; for it is God who works in you both to will and to do for His good pleasure" (Philippians 2:12, 13). Paraphrased, Paul said, "You work out your salvation because God is at work in you." You work; God works.

This participation of the Christian in divine energies is never seen as a one-time, past experience. It's dynamic. It must be a continuous experience, a constant hookup with God. God doesn't infuse us with a measure of grace and send us off to do battle while our tickers run down. God is continually supplying grace, the very grace we need, even as we do what He calls upon us to do. Remember the promise of Christ, "And lo, I am with you always, even to the end of the age" (Matthew 28:20).

A perfect illustration of cooperation

The miracle of Jesus healing the man at the pool of Bethesda in Jerusalem provides a perfect example of "co-operation" (John 5:1-9). The man had been sick for thirty-eight years. Jesus said to the sick man, "Arise, take up your bed and walk." And the man did!

This miracle peeved certain of the Jews because Jesus had healed the man on the Sabbath—and because Jesus was claiming God as His own Father. The issue became so heated that those particular religious leaders actually wanted to kill Jesus (John 5:18). In the course of the discussion between

Jesus and the Jews over the matter we can gain some revealing insights into how Jesus cooperated with His Father—and thus how we can cooperate with Him.

In replying to His accusers Jesus said: "Most assuredly, I say to you, the Son can do nothing of Himself, but what He sees the Father do; for whatever He does, the Son also does in like manner. For the Father loves the Son, and shows Him all things that He Himself does; and He will show Him greater works than these, that you may marvel" (John 5:19, 20).

Who healed the man at the pool that day?

There are two correct answers: the Father did, and the Son did. There was a cooperation between Father and Son, a working together. The Father shows the Son what He is doing, and the Son does it likewise. Jesus was not a passive channel through which the Father worked. Indeed the Father worked, but so did the Son.

So it is with those in union with Him. We are to be actively involved in doing what God has for us to do—that for which He empowers us. No longer are we powerless as we once were. Union with Christ in the Spirit gives us strength. Christ is in us, and we are in Christ. He works in us, and we work because He strengthens us.

But there must be an important word of caution. Participation in the qualities or energies of the divine nature is not a mental process—a mental mastery of a doctrinal position alone. A union with Christ that is only mentally conceived is pointless and has no power whatsoever. There is benefit in understanding these things, but understanding alone can't produce their reality in our experience. It behooves us then to actively exercise this great grace as much as is possible.

There is a growing process here. Remember Saint Peter

said, "If these qualities are yours and are abounding . . ." We aren't capable of exercising all the strength of Christ on the first day of our union with Him. But we grow and develop in that union. We build "spiritual muscle" and press on, increasing in strength.

Chapter Nine

PERSONAL COMMUNION WITH THE PERSONAL GOD

That which we have seen and heard we declare to you, that you also may have fellowship with us; and truly our fellowship is with the Father and with His Son Jesus Christ. —*I John 1:3*

Union with Christ in His glorified human nature is the supply source for victory in the unseen warfare. This is not, however, a union with an impersonal "force." It is union with our Lord and God and Savior Jesus Christ. It is therefore personal communion with God which is the theme of this chapter.

God made us to have communion with Him, and that communion should be normative to every Christian. The verb *commune* means, "to converse intimately." The opportunity to converse intimately with God has been granted to those who seek Him, and it is especially important to the "set of the heart" in the spiritual battle.

Communion with All Three Persons

First of all, communion with God is not to be limited to Christ. I've often heard the comment, "I need to spend time with the Lord." That's good, but if communion doesn't include the Father and the Holy Spirit, there's something wrong in that person's relationship to God. Communion that stops with Jesus is not the communion He came to establish. He came to introduce us to the Father—in fact, to know and converse intimately in two-way dialogue with the Father, Himself, and the Holy Spirit.

Second, communion with God is not a matter of reaching outward to a distant deity. Communion with God occurs within us. Any doubt of the possibility of communion with the Holy Trinity is dispelled by Jesus' teaching to His disciples the night of the Last Supper. There He assured His disciples that those who believe in Him would have all three persons of the Trinity within them. He spoke of the Holy Spirit being in them: "And I will pray the Father, and He will give you another Helper, that He may abide with you forever, even the Spirit of truth, whom the world cannot receive, because it neither sees Him nor knows Him; but you know Him, for He dwells with you and will be in you" (John 14:16, 17). That leaves no question about the Holy Spirit's presence in the Christian.

Then he quickly went on to include His own presence, and that of His Father, in believers: "I will not leave you orphans; I will come to you . . . If anyone loves Me, he will keep My word; and My Father will love him, and We will come to him and make Our home with him" (John 14:18, 23). This is no description of an impersonal nature residing in us. This is personal—the Father, the Son, and the Holy Spirit, all three, taking up residence in the Christian.

Third, communion with divine persons of the Trinity is possible with all three persons distinctly and without confusion. They are to be addressed distinctly and personally. They speak and they can be spoken to. Their names should not be interchanged indiscriminately either. Confusion in using their names confesses something is not real about the relationship.

I have five sons. Someone might be introduced to them all at the same time. He would obviously be aware they are distinct persons. But, until he conversed with each one personally, he would never know my sons personally. They would just be "the Braun boys," not Dan, Gary, Tim, Tom, and Peter. He may know them, but he doesn't know them personally. And similarly, it is through personal communion with the persons of the Trinity that those persons are personally known.

Don't settle for a relationship with the Trinity that is distant, impersonal, or confused. That would be a tragedy, since they have come to dwell in you to converse intimately with you.

Of course, as in any personal relationship, it takes time to build a mature personal relationship with God. Communion with God involves a life-long growing process.

The Consequences of Personal Communion with God

Many benefits result from communion with God. Here briefly summarized are four that are important.

1) In communion with God you can truly *know* the Father, Son, and Holy Spirit.

The Son of God came to make the Father known. Jesus, in His prayer to His Father on the night on which He was betrayed, said, "And this is eternal life, that they may know You, the only true God, and Jesus Christ whom You have sent" (John 17:3). Eternal life is knowing both the Father and Christ. We're forever hearing people talk about coming to know Christ personally, and equating that with salvation. But when was the last time you heard someone ask if you've ever come to know the Father personally?

There is, of course, a difference between knowing and communing personally with the persons of the Trinity and knowing facts about them. True facts about them can be known, and they are not unimportant. But knowing facts about the divine persons isn't knowing them personally. John the Beloved, Jesus' disciple, and a man who experienced communion with God wrote, "That which we have seen and heard we declare to you, that you also may have fellowship [communion] with us; and truly our fellowship [communion] is with the Father and with His Son Jesus Christ" (I John 1:3). And Saint Paul wrote that benediction we've heard so many times, "The grace of the Lord Jesus Christ, and the love of God, and the communion of the Holy Spirit, be with you all" (II Corinthians 13:14). They aren't speaking of data about the Trinity; they're speaking of real experience.

2) In communion with God you can receive *comfort* in your battle against sin.

God's presence in us gives comfort and strength when we are in the thick of the fight. Jesus guaranteed there would be tribulation in the world (John 16:33). But He also promised He would be ever with us: "And lo, I am with you always, even to the end of the age" (Matthew 28:20). That's comfort. And

He called the Holy Spirit "another comforter," assuring us the Holy Spirit would be with us forever (John 14:16). That's comfort. And Saint Paul writes, "Blessed be the God and Father of our Lord Jesus Christ, the Father of mercies and God of all comfort; who comforts us in all our tribulation" (II Corinthians 1:3, 4). That is comfort. Yes, there is comfort from the Son, the Spirit, and the Father.

Having equipped us with His divine energies, God does not leave us alone in battle. He personally accompanies us and comforts us—and strengthens us as well. This makes God's comfort constant. It is not to be an on-again off-again matter. Communion is dynamic, it's constant, and thus so is the comfort. That comfort is a great benefit of on-going communion with God.

3) In communion with God you can receive personal *guidance* in life as a Christian.

"For as many as are led by the Spirit of God, these are the sons of God," said Paul to the Romans (Romans 8:14). And he told the Thessalonians, "Now may our God and Father Himself, and our Lord Jesus Christ, direct our way to you" (I Thessalonians 3:11). Personal direction from God is available to us through His abiding in us. Don't confuse this guidance with direction we gain from reading the Bible. The Scriptures do have instructions, but invaluable as they are in themselves, they are not personal. The Bible is not a person; it is not a fourth person of the Trinity; it *cannot* give personal direction. The Holy Trinity gives personal direction—often using the Scriptures to direct us.

God's guidance, as with communion and comfort, is not intended to be sporadic. It's continual. It's actually going on in you all the time. Sometimes we are not conscious of it;

we're often not aware of it because our minds are occupied with so much else.

Several years ago I learned a wonderful prayer that came from the Orthodox Metropolitan of Moscow, who died about 1867. It is a prayer for God's guidance.

O Lord, grant me to greet the coming day in peace. Help me in all things to rely upon Your holy will. In every hour of the day reveal Your will to me. Bless my dealings with all who surround me. Teach me to treat all that comes to me throughout this day with peace of soul and firm conviction that Your will governs all. In all my deeds and words, guide my thoughts and feelings. In unforeseen events, let me not forget that all are sent by You. Teach me to act firmly and wisely without embittering and embarrassing others. Give me strength to bear the fatigue of the coming day with all that it shall bring. Direct my will, teach me to pray, pray in me Yourself. Amen.

That is guidance through communion. It's on-going, never-ceasing. It is awareness that God is always at work within us, not just when we turn to Him. Nothing happens to the children of God that the Father is not aware of and directly involved in. God does direct our lives. In communion with God we become aware of His hand on us and in us and even come to understand what His purpose is for us in the circumstances of our lives.

4) In communion with God you can be personally *taught* by God.

God personally teaches those in whom He dwells. On the

night of the Last Supper, Jesus told His disciples, "I still have many more things to say to you, but you cannot bear them now. However, when He, the Spirit of truth, has come, He will guide you into all the truth; for He will not speak on His own authority, but whatever He hears He will speak; and He will tell you things to come" (John 16:12, 13). Earlier He had said, "But the Helper, the Holy Spirit, whom the Father will send in My name, He will teach you all things, and bring to your remembrance all that I said to you" (John 14:26). We are taught personally from the Father, through the Son, in the Spirit.

Ways We Commune with God

Having considered four results of communion with God, now contemplate some of the ways in which we may commune with Him. There are many. Here are some which are basic.

1) There is communion with God in the corporate worship of the Church.

Public or corporate worship is intended to be infinitely more than a religious observance, a religious performance. In worship, the people of God come together to meet personally with the All Holy Trinity and to render praise and thanksgiving to God with all their hearts. True worship includes true communion with God.

The singing of psalms, hymns, and spiritual songs, the prayers, the reading of the Scriptures, the sermon, and Holy Communion—these all relate to communion with God. In fact, the entire worship service of the Orthodox Church, the Divine Liturgy, is actually a personal dialogue between the worshipers corporately and the All Holy Trinity. And it's not

"I praise You" but "We praise You." It is corporate and personal.

Every hymn and every prayer of the Liturgy is addressed to one of the persons of the Holy Trinity. God is never addressed in catch-all generalizations. We address the Father specifically, the Son specifically, or the Holy Spirit specifically. The very heart of the Liturgy, the Eucharistic prayer, for example, is addressed specifically to the Father. This doesn't insure that everyone in the Church communes with God, by the way. But it does guarantee the availability of that communion.

Communion with God in the corporate worship of the Church should be so evident that even a casual, unbelieving observer will be astonished at the Church's awareness of the presence of God. And this is not because of entertaining music or eloquent preaching—you can have those without God—but because God is personally present.

Communion with God at Holy Communion is the center core, the very heart, of worship. It is an experience much of modern Christianity is hardly aware of. Even when observed, for many the Lord's Supper is a history lesson in the memory, calling to mind the death of the Lord. That is a profitable form of cognitive thought, but it is not communion. Rather, at the Lord's Table we are to "touch" God. We are to "taste and see that the Lord is good." We are to be caught up in the reality of God's presence with us. Therein is the communion in worship.

2) There is also communion with God when not in the public worship of the Church.

Notice I didn't use the expression "private worship." There is personal worship, but no such thing as private worship. You can't have a private audience with God, for God is never alone. The cherubim and the seraphim—six-winged, many-eyed, soaring high on their wings—are there, as are all the angels of God, and the saints of all the ages. You can't have "a time alone with the Lord," not with the God of heaven and earth. But don't be discouraged by that. The reality is far greater. It helps make worship of God when not in Church a richer opportunity for communion with God.

Prayer, the reading of Scripture, the reading of good Christian literature, and the singing of the Psalms are some of the channels through which communion with God may be experienced when not in the public worship of the Church. But so are stillness and wordlessness. There are many ways we can commune with God.

3) There is also communion with God in communion with others in communion with God.

In the great mystery of God, He often communes with us through each other in the Church. Saint John wrote, "That which we have seen and heard we declare to you, that you also may have fellowship with us; and truly our fellowship is with the Father and with His Son Jesus Christ" (I John 1:3). The Church, the body of Christ, is made up of many members. Each member has a service to render to the whole. The Holy Spirit personally directs each willing part of the body in his contribution to the whole body. From that issues communion with God.

Comfort from God, for example, often comes to us through others in communion with God. "Blessed be the God and Father of our Lord Jesus Christ, the Father of mercies and God of all comfort; who comforts us in all our tribulation, that we may be able to comfort those who are in any trouble, with the comfort with which we ourselves are comforted by God" (II Corinthians 1:3, 4). We may comfort others, or be comforted by others, with the very comfort with which God comforts. It remains the comfort of God; it is personal through His people.

These are but three examples of how we can personally commune with God—Father, Son, and Holy Spirit. They are ours to take advantage of. All of them need to be a part of our lives.

Communion with God is invaluable for succeeding in spiritual combat. It is one of the highest privileges He, in His great grace, has given to His people.

PART III

CHRIST OUR VICTORY

Chapter Ten

THE ACTION PLAN

Almighty God who in wisdom made all creation; O You, who for Your ineffable providence and the greatness of Your goodness, brought us these most solemn days, for the purification of our souls and bodies by abstinence from passion, and for hope of resurrection; grant us too, O Good One, that we may fight the good fight, finish the course of the fast, and keep the Faith intact, bruising the heads of the invisible dragons, appearing victorious over sin, and arriving at the worship of Your holy resurrection without condemnation; for Your most honored and exalted Name is blessed and glorified, O Father, Son, and Holy Spirit, now and ever, and unto ages of ages. Amen. —From a prayer on the first Saturday of the Great Fast of Lent

So far we have reviewed some of the problems encountered in our warfare against sin and the devil. For a solution to those problems we have focused on what *God* has done for *us* in the incarnation. In that light we've discussed union with

Jesus Christ in His glorified humanity—how God brings us into that union through baptism and nurtures us in that union through Holy Communion—and we've also discussed our personal communion with all three members of the Holy Trinity.

Apart from this union with Christ and personal communion with the Trinity there is no possibility of victory in the unseen warfare. It's not even a contest. God has provided us with everything we need, and given us every means to overcome the enemy fully and completely.

We cannot, however, consider the battle over simply because we know these facts. Even participation in the sacraments will not assure victory. The Christian life is not a passive life. Armed with the knowledge of what God has done for us, and enlivened by participation in the sacramental life of His Church, there are still things *we* must do in order to "work out our own salvation."

As mentioned in chapter eight, we are to be neither bootstrappers nor channels-only Christians, but co-operators with God. We need to know what God expects from us in this spiritual battle and work together with Him to exercise our spiritual muscles in preparation for the fight. This chapter is therefore about our part in the unseen warfare, and the action plan we need to assimilate into our lives.

One of the more foolish things I can imagine is for an army to thrust fresh recruits immediately into combat with no knowledge, instruction, and training about their enemy and how to fight. It ceases being foolish, however, and becomes sick when they are then promised glorious victory.

Yet something akin to that is happening to literally millions of Christians today. They have been challenged to follow

Christ and promised a wonderful and abundant life, but they aren't prepared for inevitable spiritual combat. They need information about the conflict that will ensue and how to contend with it. Many will fall as casualties without that help. Jesus thoroughly prepared His disciples for all they would encounter after His ascension. He guaranteed them, "In the world you will have tribulation" (John 16:33). And Saint Paul, the "battle trainer" of Timothy wrote the latter, "Fight the good fight of faith" (I Timothy 6:12). Saint James wrote, "Count it all joy when you fall into various trials" (James 1:2). No doubt was left as to what trouble lay ahead.

The shocker for many of us is that we were told the Christian life included a battle, but we were not equipped to fight. And remember—it was to be relatively easy anyway. Just a prayer or two (sometimes a very trite prayer, no less), or a Bible verse. Then came the harsh realities of war, and we weren't prepared. We need to know we've got a fight on our hands and how to contend in it. Fun singing, some Bible verses and some prayers are good but they are far from enough preparation.

How I wish someone would have warned me that summer I first consciously decided to follow Christ. I still would have accepted the challenge, but I honestly believe there would have been much less confusion and grief for me and far greater progress had I been better prepared. There were things I needed to do I didn't even know about, and lacking that basic training, I was particularly easy prey for my enemy.

Preparation Tested for Two Thousand Years

The Scriptures testify that there are actions which are essential if we are to win. We don't have to guess what to do.

We don't have to experiment. The Church now has two thousand years of battle knowledge behind her. We can trust what she's learned about these actions.

Preparation begins with some rigorous training. None of it comes automatically to us. In the Gospels, Jesus teaches there are four specific actions we must take if we are to successfully engage in the battle between darkness and light: prayer, fasting, almsgiving, and virtuous living.

Prayer

Prayer is primary for any Christian who seeks to follow Christ. Jesus commanded us to pray, and specifically with respect to temptation (Matthew 26:41). Prayer needs to be examined from the perspective of its two principle applications.

Corporate prayer

First, there is the common prayer of the assembled Church, particularly in the Eucharistic worship. I'll say it dogmatically: absent yourself from it and you're a guaranteed loser. Prayer together is at least as important as prayer when you're alone. And the more we pray together the more we'll pray alone.

Look, prayer takes discipline. It is *difficult.* In a sense prayer is often part of the battle itself! If you're not in a spiritual battle at the moment, just start praying consistently and you'll be in the fray in a very short time! It seems as though every demon of hell comes out to do battle with us when we pray!

Personal prayer

Second, in addition to the corporate prayer of the Church, there is your personal prayer. We need to pray—even without ceasing (I Thessalonians 5:17). The question so often asked is, how are we to pray? It's the same question Jesus' disciples asked Him. His response is as true now as it was then: "When you pray, say . . ." (Luke 11:2). Then He gave us the prayer we call "The Lord's Prayer." Again, this prayer is not optional; it is commanded by Christ. The Lord's Prayer is an essential part of almost all worship and it is the model for all prayer.

Many Christians I've known, however, seldom use the Lord's Prayer when they pray. Perhaps their congregation uses it on Sundays, but they almost never pray it at any other time. That's not taking Jesus' instruction seriously. The Lord's Prayer should be on our lips constantly. From the earliest days of the Church, Christians have formed their personal prayer around the Lord's Prayer. They have surrounded it with other prayers, starting with the Psalms, and their own prayers, but the Lord's Prayer has always been present. Along the line, however, sometime after the beginning of the Reformation, suspicion arose over the use of written prayers. In some circles they were judged to be unspiritual.

As difficult as it is to believe—against what Jesus and the Apostles taught and practiced—there are professing Christians who believe that repeating the words of a written prayer is improper and not actually praying. (This same body of people, though, find nothing wrong with a memorized hymn!) They won't even pray the Lord's Prayer! I know; I was there myself! That's an indictment of the Lord.

Not only did Jesus teach such prayer, He *practiced* it. We know for an indisputable fact He used the Psalms. And we know as well that the Apostles prayed "set" prayers. In Acts 2:42, it is recorded, "And they continued steadfastly in the apostle's doctrine and fellowship, in the breaking of bread, and in prayers." An accurate rendering of that last phrase would show the Apostles continued steadfastly in *the* prayers.

Spontaneous prayer

Spontaneous prayer is valuable, but if it's the full extent of your prayer, you don't "have a prayer" in your war with sin. Few of us can, or will, effectively put into words the desires and needs of our hearts. And we certainly do not do it as well as the Lord's Prayer, the Psalms, and the proven prayers of the Church.

But when you do pray spontaneously, *after* you pray the Lord's Prayer and other established prayers of the Church, great wisdom should be observed. Why? So much spontaneous prayer is trite—an insult to God. Saint Isaac the Syrian, who lived in the seventh century, cautioned us about our prayer:

> Do not become foolish in your petitions, lest you insult God. . . . Become wise in your prayers that you may be accounted worthy of glorious things. Seek what is honorable from Him who gives ungrudgingly. . . .
> Solomon asked for wisdom and with it he received an earthly kingdom, inasmuch as he asked wisely of the Great King Himself. Elisha asked for a double portion of the grace of the Spirit that abode on his teacher, and by no means failed in his request. For he that requests contemptible things of a king brings contempt upon the latter's honor. . . . Present your petitions to God so as to accord with His glory . . .
> For if a man should beseech the king for a measure of dung, he not only dishonors himself by his miser-

able petition (since he has shown great lack of sense), but also he has heaped insult upon the king because of what he asked for. Even so, he that seeks earthly things from God in his prayers does the same. For lo, angels and archangels, who are the King's great officials, are gazing steadfastly upon you at the time of your prayer to see what petition you will make of their Master. And they are astonished and exultant whenever they behold one who is made of earth forsake his dunghill and ask for what is heavenly (*The Ascetical Homilies of Saint Isaac the Syrian*, Homily Three).

A "rule" of prayer

Let me take it a step farther. Every Christian needs a "rule" of prayer. By that I mean a set of prayers and Scriptures you use *daily*. It needn't be long; it does need to be practiced consistently. Until you do this, you're likely in for a discouraging string of defeats both in the battle to pray and in prayer for the battle. Ask your priest or spiritual director for help in establishing a rule. Then faithfully do what is suggested. That is ordinarily the safest and best route to an effective rule of prayer.

Fasting

Fasting also is crucial for anyone who would faithfully follow Christ. The Lord said, "Can the friends of the bridegroom mourn as long as the bridegroom is with them? But the days will come when the bridegroom will be taken away from them, and then they will fast" (Matthew 9:15). He Himself fasted, and He assumed His followers would do the same. He said, "When you fast . . ." not "If you fast . . ." (Matthew 6:16).

The purpose of fasting is not to gain points with God. It is to discipline the body and to give undivided attention to God in our prayer, as opposed to our preoccupation with material things. Winners fast. Those who don't, disobey Christ and become losers in the spiritual warfare. Saint Diadochus, fifth century bishop of the Greek city of Photiki, writes:

> When heavy with over-eating, the body makes the intellect spiritless and sluggish. Likewise, when weakened by excessive abstinence, the body makes the contemplative faculty of the soul dejected and disinclined to concentrate. We should therefore regulate our food according to the condition of the body, so that it is appropriately disciplined when in good health, and adequately nourished, when weak. The body of one pursuing the spiritual way must not be enfeebled; he must have enough strength for his labours, so that the soul may be suitably purified through bodily exertion as well ("On Spiritual Knowledge," *The Philokalia, Volume I*).

As with prayer, fasting is best pursued under the direction of a spiritual guide. Overkill, to which so many of us are prone, seems appealing at first. But if we try too much, we will quit too soon. An informed pastor who knows his sheep can help keep us on the track.

There is great benefit in fasting. Saint John of the Ladder, a saintly seventh century Christian, addresses these benefits:

> Fasting ends lust, roots out bad thoughts, frees one from evil dreams; fasting makes for purity of prayer, an enlightened soul, a watchful mind, a deliverance from blindness. Fasting is the door of compunction,

humble sighing, joyful contrition, an end to chatter, an occasion for silence, a custodian of obedience, a lightening of sleep, health of the body, agent of dispassion, a remission of sins, the gate, indeed, the delight of Paradise (*The Ladder of Divine Ascent*, 14:33).

Did Saint John get a bit carried away in his enthusiasm? Not on your life. He learned this from practice in his personal experience. This was no matter of theory to him. All of us would love to have those attributes characteristic of our lives. Fasting is at least part of the route to them.

How to go about fasting

As with prayer, we don't have to "re-invent the wheel," as it were, for fasting. The Church has twenty centuries of experience fasting. It isn't complicated to lock into that experience. There are, for example, regular days—anciently established—during the week for fasting: Wednesdays and Fridays. And there are also many other special days set aside—and there are seasons for fasting, Lent being the most important. There is even help on what, if anything, to eat, and how long to fast.

First, there is the total fast. This is done before receiving Holy Communion in order: 1) to help prepare the heart for communion, and 2) that the body and blood of Christ be the first thing eaten that day. The total fast is also profitable for other times set aside for prayer.

Second, there is the partial fast. This is employed for longer periods of fasting in which a total fast is impractical or impossible. Here are four categories of foods the Christian may deny to himself: 1) meat, 2) all animal products, 3) fish with backbones, and 4) oil. Depending on circumstances and ability, the fasting Christian abstains for a time, during Lent for example, from one or more of these categories. Why? Will it earn merit with God? It has nothing to do with merit or lack of it. It does have to do with turning attention to God and the things of God. It works.

Include the Church's practice of fasting in your life, for it will be of great assistance to you as a Christian.

Almsgiving

Being a winning Christian also costs money! One place we will give it is in almsgiving. As with prayer and fasting, Jesus assumed His followers would give alms. Isn't it strange that the very word "almsgiving" is so unfamiliar to most of us? "Alms" is an old English word meaning "charity," or "something freely given for the help of the poor." Free and open-handed giving is essential if you are to grow to be like Christ our God.

Almsgiving is a private matter. We don't boast about it, announce it, or drop subtle hints about how generous we've been with the needy. The Lord said regarding almsgiving, "But when you do a charitable deed, do not let your left hand know what your right hand is doing" (Matthew 6:3).

The world is full of opportunities to help unfortunate people. We don't need a case study to determine whether a hungry person is worthy of a few dollars of our hard-earned money. Don't be a tightwad. So the guy is a bum. Remember, "For with what judgment you judge, you will be judged" (Matthew 7:2). Hungry bums need to eat. We are not so worthy ourselves, are we? If your compassion for the poor and needy doesn't bring you to give, you won't make much progress as a Christian. Saint Maximus the Confessor (c. 580-662), whose tongue was cut out and right hand cut off for speaking and writing in defense of the Faith, said of almsgiving:

> He who gives alms in imitation of God does not discriminate between the wicked and the virtuous, the just and the unjust, when providing for men's bodily needs. He gives equally to all according to their need, even though he prefers the virtuous man to the bad man because of the uprightness of his intention ("First Century On Love," no. 24, *The Philokalia*, Volume II).

We're not talking here about giving away the family fortune. (That's another subject!) But we are talking about having mercy on the needy. The New Testament is full of examples of such giving: the Magi, who no doubt financed a trip to Egypt for a needy family with a new Baby! (Matthew 2:11-15); Cornelius, the Centurion (Acts 10:1, 2); the Good Samaritan (Luke 10:30-37); and the Christians outside of Judea for the Christians living in Judea (I Corinthians 16:1*ff.*), to name but a few.

Throughout the centuries the Church has believed that the person who loves God and is growing in that love is an open-handed giver. Again, Saint Maximus writes, "A person who loves God will certainly love his neighbor as well, and such a person cannot hoard money, but distributes it in a way befitting God, being generous to everyone in need."

Almsgiving is essential training for the battle—even if you yourself are poor!

A Virtuous Life

Virtue is part of the preparation of a Christian for battle against sin. The lack of virtue is a mark of defeat. Strangely, virtuous living has come on hard times in some circles because of the fear someone might think he is earning merit with God for salvation by being virtuous. Virtue doesn't earn salvation, but it is a vital part of waging spiritual war. You can't ignore virtue and succeed in spiritual combat.

Saint Philothios, who lived about a thousand years ago, said:

Our Savior says: "Watch yourselves, lest your hearts be weighed down by dissipation, drunkenness, and worldly cares" (Luke 21:34). And Saint Paul says the person engaged in spiritual warfare exercises self-control in all things (I Corinthians 9:25).

Aware of all that is said to us in divine Scripture, let us lead our life with self-control, especially in regard to food. Let us accustom our body to virtuous and orderly habits, nourishing it with moderation. For in this way the upsurges of the soul's desiring power are more easily calmed . . . For those with experience regard virtue as consisting in all-inclusive self-control, that is, in avoidance of every kind of evil (*The Philokalia*, Volume III).

What is our guide to virtue? First, the Ten Commandments. People in union with Christ must not settle for living at a lower level of virtue than that set forth in the Old Testament. Jesus made that clear in our second guide to virtue, the Sermon on the Mount. Some have written off that Sermon as representing an impossible ideal. Others seek means to avoid its uncomfortable application. But since the Day of Pentecost, the Church has seen the Sermon on the Mount as setting the ideal goal of conduct for the Christian life.

There are other guides to virtue as well. One ancient writer, thought by some to have been Saint John of Damascus, listed thirty-three virtues of the soul: "faith, hope, love, prayer, humility, gentleness, long-suffering, forbearance, kindness, freedom from anger, knowledge of God, cheerfulness, simplicity, calmness, sincerity, freedom from vanity, freedom from pride, absence of envy, honesty, freedom from avarice, compassion, mercifulness, generosity, fearlessness, freedom from dejection, deep compunction, modesty, reverence, desire for the blessings held in store, longing for the kingdom of God, and aspiration for divine sonship." That's not a bad list for starters!

But suppose we don't measure up? What if we fail in virtue? I understand failure. I'm an expert in that field, with lots of practice. But I'm also learning about getting back up. We are not to accept failure as normative. God does forgive us when we fail. But after any failure we must set our eyes on the goal, get up, and strive once more for virtue.

Aim at virtue. In Christ, there can be for us steady progress toward it.

We have made but a beginning here in setting forth some of the essential actions for spiritual strength. Pursue these if you desire to build some "spiritual muscle." They are "basic training" in preparation for being a soldier of Christ.

Chapter Eleven

A BATTLE CALL

Let us go forth in peace, in the name of the Lord. —*From the Divine Liturgy of Saint John Chrysostom*

Enough for knowing!

All the knowledge of God's provision for us in Christ, valuable as it is, becomes useless if we don't go on the offensive and into the battle. It's actually counterproductive. We would do better to be ignorant of what God has done than to know yet do nothing. In fact, doing nothing is perhaps the greatest spiritual defeat of all in this life.

I want to challenge you to get into the thick of the battle. And there are four things to encourage you into accepting that challenge. First is the remembrance of God. Second is the knowledge you're not alone in the war. Third, your victory in the battle can change the world around you. And fourth, there is a reward in heaven for those who war well.

The Remembrance of God

Have you ever gone for days with just one primary thought dominating your mind? Did this affect the way you lived and acted? You bet it did!

I remember the week I began falling in love with the lady who has become my wife. Speaking somewhat romantically, I would say I didn't think about anything else or anyone else for days. That's not really quite true. I thought about other things and people, but not without my thoughts of her affecting what and how I thought, and how well I paid attention to what I was doing at any given time. Now, after thirty-eight years of marriage, I still think of her, but with more control, more balance. I've actually gained a measure of sanity with regard to her.

I remember I'm married. Two items—my wife and the fact I'm married to her—reside unceasingly in my memory, and they affect how I live. In a major way! That memory determines how I spend my time, how I relate to other women, even how I relate to my children and grandchildren. It's a comfortable memory, not a threat, and it does impact my action. Believe me when I say that I've never forgotten once in all those years that I'm married.

What I've described is a limited picture of how it should be with our memory of God. For remembrance of Him greatly affects our lives.

But more than that, in a very real sense the remembrance of God brings life to us from God. Memory is a conduit, as it were, for the heat of the fire to come into the sword—to hearken back once again to that illustration.

In the biblical concept of memory, life itself is abiding in the memory of God. God's memory is real, not imagination, and if I exist in His memory I'm alive and real. Out of His memory I'm dead.

Our memory of God is our response in love to His memory

of us. The Psalmist writes, "When I remember You on my bed, I meditate on You in the night watches" (Psalm 63:6). To forget God is to be cut off from Him, from His life.

How many times in my life I've heard Christians almost cry out, "O how I wish I could go through the day thinking about God! But I don't. I work the whole day without even a thought of Him." That plight must be remedied if we are to effectively accept the challenge to spiritual battle. Otherwise, you will miss the impact of your memory of Him in the very times you need it most. Discouragement is the only alternative.

Understand I am not suggesting you go into battle remembering the things in this book. That might be helpful, but what I'm urging is that you go into battle with the memory of God because in memory you will find life and strength in the battle.

But how do we do it? How do we remember God?

Christ is the answer to our holding God in our memory. Why? Because in His life as the incarnate Son of God, as a man He perfectly remembered God, and still does for that matter. And since we are to participate in His perfect humanity, we have access to His perfect memory of God.

It is in the reality of this remembrance of God that the Christian life becomes dynamic, because it makes the past present—current. The cross becomes a present reality. The resurrection is a present reality. The ascension is a present reality. The work of the Holy Spirit in our lives is a present reality. Take God out of our memory and we fall away. At least for a time these things become history to us. Life gets stale, and we're struggling to find life.

The action plan from the last chapter helps to keep us remembering God. Continual prayer, fasting—with its continual awareness of hunger—and almsgiving help tune us into that memory, or prevent us from falling from it. These are only the beginning of ways, but they are the place to start.

In the thick of the fight, there is perhaps no greater weapon than the memory of God and all that He is to us. There's battle power in it. It is essential to our growing in union with Him into His likeness.

You are Not Alone

It's hard to fight when you think you're alone or outnumbered. Many of us have ventured into battle almost like private citizens. There was no sense of an army, in this case the spiritual community, the Church.

That aloneness has disaster written all over it. Few have warred well alone, and most of them only by necessity. But those of us who live surrounded constantly by people and confronting busy daily schedules need the encouragement of battling shoulder to shoulder with others. There is strength in numbers, and there's even strength in knowing there are numbers out there.

But the value of the spiritual community goes far beyond numbers. There is prayer for one another in a true spiritual community, and that is utterly essential. We need to pray for others in respect to their battles, and we need to be prayed for as well. Through prayer we can actually join in with others to help them gain strength in the fight, far across the miles.

Though there are psychological values to being together, I'm not focusing on those. I have in mind here real strength. Something that actually is. We Christians possess the same life in Christ, a common life, joined to Him in and through the Spirit. Because of this we carry the Church with us wherever we go.

Then there is the totality of the life of the Church in a given place—the day-by-day living as a Christian community. There's great strength in that. At the end of the Divine Liturgy, the Sunday service of the Orthodox Church, after we have all entered heaven to worship God and have partaken of His body and blood, the priest says, "Let us go forth in peace in the name of the Lord." Then, and only then, are we ready to go back out to the fight. But go forth is what we must do, now strengthened. There is spiritual strength in the life of the Christian community.

Transformation of the Culture Around Us

The spiritual warfare around us gets bewilderingly complicated at times because of the increasing moral corruption of the culture in which we live. The intensity of temptation increases because of the growing rebellion of the culture against God. Sexual temptations, for example, are more numerous and complex for our kids than they were for us. The same is true with the drug scene, just to name two issues.

So what are we to do? Just assume there is no hope and kick back for the duration, caving into the notion that things can't get anything but worse? That's depressing.

Things can change. People living in God can impact the culture around them. I'm not talking about changing laws. I'm talking about changing people and their basic attitudes. Life begets life, and where Christians are present and live in Christ, there is the possibility that those around them will catch that life too.

We can, as Christians together, experience a winning fight against sin, death, and Satan, and have an impact. It's happened many times before in history. It can happen in our time as well.

Great is Your Reward in Heaven

There are times you feel it's just not worth all the effort and pain to go through the spiritual battles. Right? I have often succumbed to that temptation to discouragement. I'll grant you that things really do get difficult. At times it seems as if there is no end in sight. So you win a few rounds. What are they amongst so many battles in a seemingly endless war?

Be encouraged. The war is not forever. It "ain't over 'til it's over," *but it will be over!* Completely over—never to start again. And the reward for waging a good fight is eternal.

After Jesus said, "Blessed are you when they revile and persecute you, and say all kinds of evil against you falsely for My sake," He immediately added, "Rejoice and be exceedingly glad, for great is your reward in heaven, for so they persecuted the prophets who were before you" (Matthew 5:11, 12).

There is heaven. There is everlasting life. This is the time beyond time when there will be no more death, no more mourning, no more crying, and no more pain (Revelation 21:4). The wars will be over and the spoils of victory will be sweet. Such reward brings great motivation to us as we are in the midst of the fight.

Conclusion

Spiritual warfare is a given in Christian living, if the latter is taken seriously. The personal experience I related in chapter one may be far removed from yours, but reality of the war will be the same for all serious Christians.

Pat answers and clever schemes for "victorious living" are useless. All the schemes in the world for winning spiritual wars end in escalating defeats. What has been offered in this book is no secret, no shortcut, no scheme. It's simply the report of centuries-long, tried and proven spiritual battle tradition.

It begins with a solid understanding and experience of God. That necessarily calls for us to lay a hold on the incarnation of Jesus Christ and what that means for us in relation to the forgiveness of our sins. But we are also united to Christ and nourished by Him through the sacraments, the mysteries, to which we have access in the Church, drawing on those divine energies made available to us in Christ. In addition we must also continually cooperate with God by actively pursuing a godly life through prayer, fasting, almsgiving, and virtuous living.

All of these are vital to successful spiritual warfare. There are no formulas, no "keys." It is simply a matter of living life as God has given it to us in Christ.

John, the Apostle of Jesus, at the end of his life wrote, "I write to you, young men, because you have overcome the wicked one" (I John 2:13). Victory in spiritual battle is not impossible. It is assumed in that statement. It is in fact a reality.

May this same overcoming of sin, Satan, and death be a reality in the lives of all of God's people who seek to serve Him and walk in His way.